101 Ways to
Do More With Your Dog!

QUARRY

101 Ways to
Do More With Your Dog!

Make Your Dog a Superdog with
Sports • Games • Exercises • Tricks
Challenges • Crafts • Bonding

Kyra Sundance

BEVERLY MASSACHUSETTS

QUARRY BOOKS

First published in the United States of America by
Quarry Books, a member of
Quayside Publishing Group
100 Cummings Center
Suite 406-L
Beverly, Massachusetts 01915-6101
Telephone: (978) 282-9590
Fax: (978) 283-2742
www.quarrybooks.com

Library of Congress Cataloging-in-Publication Data

Sundance, Kyra.
  101 ways to do more with your dog : make your dog a superdog with sports, games, exercises, tricks, mental challenges, crafts, and bonding / Kyra Sundance.
       p. cm.
  Includes bibliographical references and index.
  ISBN-13: 978-1-59253-642-9 (alk. paper)
  ISBN-10: 1-59253-642-5 (alk. paper)
  1. Dogs–Training. I. Title. II. Title: One hundred one ways to do more with your dog. III. Title: Hundred and one ways to do more with your dog.
  SF431.S863 2010
  636.7–dc22

                                                      2010020249

ISBN-13: 978-1-59253-642-9
ISBN-10: 1-59253-642-5

10 9 8 7 6 5 4 3 2

Design: Sundance MediaCom (www.sundancemediacom.com)
"Do More with Your Dog!" is a registered trademark of Kyra Sundance (www.kyra.com).

Due to differing conditions, materials, and skill levels, the publisher and various manufacturers disclaim any liability for unsatisfactory results or injury due to improper use of tools, materials, or information.

Recipe on page 199, courtesy of Quarry Books.

Cover photography by Nick Saglimbeni (www.slickforce.com)
Back cover photography: © Gonzalo Azumendi/agefotostock.com (top, left); Karen Hocker Photography (top, middle); Steven Donahue/See Spot Run Photography (top, right); Christian Arias (bottom, right)

Printed in Singapore

He is your friend, your partner, your defender, your dog. You are his life, his love, his leader. He will be yours, faithful and true, to the last beat of his heart. You owe it to him to be worthy of such devotion.

— Anonymous

DoMoreWithYourDog.com

CONTENTS

Do More
With Your Dog!

DoMoreWithYourDog.com

AUTHOR'S NOTE

Wow! Look at all these cool dog sports and activities!

I've trained and competed in tons of dog sports and activities (everything from competitive obedience, to land mushing, to animal acting). But after writing this book, I now have a whole new list of things I want to learn and try with my dogs! I want to sign up for a dog surfing lesson, take a doga class, get out my cross-country skis and try skijoring, and teach my dog to paint!

Inspired during the writing of this book, I took my Weimaraners (pointing breed) to a sheep herding lesson. Chalcy tried to bite the sheep, and puppy Jadie thought they were giant fleece squeak toys! Neither (not surprisingly) showed much herding instinct. It's not a sport we will ever be good enough to compete in, but it was a great outdoor romp, and we laughed, and shared an experience, and came home with good story.

Trying new things with your dog is not only good for your dog—it's good for you. Motivation to exercise and to get out of your comfort zone is always a struggle, but dogs have a way of making the activities we share with them more fun.

Finding which sports best suit you and your dog is a challenge. Most often it is your dog that will make the clear choice and you that follows his lead. Much of what we do with our dogs is out of the pure joy of watching them do what makes them happy and in some cases, comes naturally to them.

As you look through this book, be sure to check out the features by experts in each sport. Through the course of my dog career, I've befriended some of the greatest dog sportsmen in the world. Many of these people are world-class competitors and at the top of their fields. As I interviewed each person, I was repeatedly amazed at the things that came out of their mouths. These people haven't gotten to the top by accident. Listen to their insights.

I hope this book inspires you to "Do More With Your Dog!®"

Bonds are built through shared experiences: physical, mental, and emotional.

Don't be so focused on the goal that you miss the joys of the journey!

He's YOUR dog, and his success need only be measured in YOUR eyes.

A GREAT DOG RELATIONSHIP

You're a "dog person." And as a dog person, you try to make a good life for your dog, and you like to involve your dog in your life wherever your can. You strive for not just a relationship with your dog but a *great* relationship with your dog.

A great relationship does not necessarily begin when you first bring home a puppy or when you first sign up for a training class.

- Bonds are built through shared experiences: physical, mental, and emotional.

- Great relationships are built through work, collaboration, challenge, inspiration, exhilaration in goals met, and consolation in goals missed. They are built through communication and reliably meeting one another's needs.

Some of this book's readers are pet owners, some are beginners in dog sports, some are advanced competitors and trainers, and others merely take pleasure in their dog's companionship. However he fits into your life, there are ways you can do more with your dog—teach him a new sport, find an activity you can enjoy together, work with him, engage him, challenge him, strive for common goals, take him places with you, spend more time with him, and bond more deeply with him. These are the ways great relationships are built.

Dogs don't want to lie on the couch all day. Dogs want to be challenged and have goals to strive for. They want to be taught things, struggle with physical and mental contests, and taste sweet success!

There are 101 activities in this book, and hopefully you will be inspired to try some of them. While it's motivating to have a goal in a sport, the best thing that comes out of training your dog is the bond that develops through working together. The trust and cooperative spirit developed through this process will last a lifetime.

The rewards are in the journey and the successes are measured in the smiles, barks, and tail wags of you and your best bud. Don't be so focused on a goal that you miss the joys of the journey. This is the beginning of your pursuit of your best dog relationship!

PHYSICAL SOUNDNESS

Check With Your Veterinarian

Some of the sports in this book are physically demanding on your dog. Don't risk injury by entering into the sport unprepared. Check with your veterinarian to ensure your dog is physically sound. Be aware that excess weight on a dog will make him more prone to injury when doing a sport.

Warm Up, Stretch, Cool Down

Take your dog through warm up and cool down exercises before and after strenuous physical activity and consider massage and stretching sessions.

First, Think of Injury

Dogs are honest. They will give you what you want within the limitations of their physical and mental capabilities, and of their training. If your dog is not performing physically up to your expectations, think first of injury. Dogs hide their injuries and pain, so it may not be obvious to you. Before you get frustrated at your dog's less than optimal effort, consider if he might be sick, injured, scared, or is having difficulty with one of his senses.

A HEALTHY AND HAPPY DOG HAS HIS NEEDS FULFILLED IN FOUR AREAS:

PHYSICAL   MENTAL   SOCIAL   BONDING

PHYSICAL: A dog needs physical exercise. Exercise can come in the form of **strength training** (as in weight pulling), **endurance training** (sled dog racing), **aerobic training** (lure coursing), and **flexibility** (massage).

MENTAL: Mental challenges keep your dog sharp and engaged. A dog is mentally challenged by learning new things, by using his nose to home in on a scent, and by figuring out logic tasks.

SOCIAL: The more a dog is socialized, the more comfortable he is in his daily life. He becomes confident and at ease with new situations. A dog is socialized through positive exposure to new objects and situations.

BONDING: You are the most important person in your dog's life, and he needs to feel loved and connected with you. Bond with your dog by focusing on him, either eye-to-eye (as in training dog tricks) or side-by-side (as in agility training).

HOW TO USE THIS BOOK

Needs Fulfilment Indicator

In the upper corner of every activity page is a **needs fulfilment indicator** similar to the one pictured above. This designates which of a dog's four key needs can be *most* fulfilled by this activity.

Ideal Dogs for This Activity

Certain dog breeds, sizes, or temperaments are better suited to specific activities than others. A herding breed dog, for example, will naturally be better at the sport of herding. Some competition sports (such as terrier racing) are restricted to certain breeds. Each activity in this book includes a box with recommendations on the types of dogs that excel in it.

Gear

Just about every sport and activity uses specialized gear. Using the proper gear will not only make you more successful in the sport, but will make you feel more comfortable in participating in the sport. A **gear** section will let you know what you need for each activity.

How to Get Started

What's the first step? A **how to get started** section will give you the first steps to teaching your dog each new activity. In most cases, you can get started right away with simple lessons that begin in your home. This will give you and your dog a chance to try out the sport without the cost and effort of enrolling in a class or finding a club. If you have success with your first attempts and decide this is a sport you'd like to pursue, you will have the confidence of already having had a little experience before you enroll in a class.

Meet the Experts

Get a feel for the sport with a first-hand account of the experiences of an expert in that field, as featured in the sidebar. Experts pass along their best tips, just for you!

Resources

At the back of this book is a detailed **resources** section, which lists websites associated with the main organizations for each sport or activity.

This golden retriever makes sure to touch the yellow contact zone before jumping off the teeter totter obstacle.

Agility

Inspired by equestrian jumping courses, dog agility is a race in which the dog, guided by his handler, maneuvers through a path of obstacles. Obstacles include jumps, teeter totters, weave poles, tire jumps, A-frames, dogwalks (elevated planks), tunnels, and pause tables. In every competition, obstacles are arranged in a different order within a roughly 100' x 100' (30 x 30 m) course. Shortly before the start of competition, handlers receive a **course map** which instructs them on the path the dog is to take through the obstacles. Handlers may walk the course and plan their strategy, but dogs may not enter the ring until it is their turn to compete.

One dog and handler run the course at a time, competing for the fastest time. The handler runs alongside her dog but may not touch her dog nor the obstacles. She guides him with verbal commands and body language. Fault deductions occur for mistakes such as the dog running past the correct obstacle. The dog is eliminated for major faults such as knocking a bar on a jump, taking an obstacle out of order, or flying off an obstacle such as the teeter-totter without touching the yellow bottom portion of it (called the **contact zone**). The goal of every handler is to have a **clean run**, with no faults.

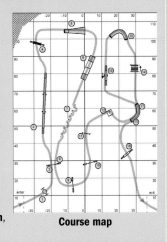

Course map

GEAR

For safety reasons, dogs generally run "naked" without a collar. **Tug leashes** are often used to reward the dog with a game at the finish.

HOW TO GET STARTED

Teach your dog to stop on the contact zone by directing his attention to a marker with a food treat at the bottom of a plank.

MEET SUSAN GARRETT
AGILITY WORLD CHAMPION, ONTARIO, CANADA

"Agility is all about dog and handler teamwork, even at the novice levels. The teamwork that develops through agility training will strengthen your bond with your dog.

"Before you start obstacle training, work on foundation skills at home: train a good recall and a retrieve. Avoid injuries by getting your dog into good physical shape; you should be easily able to feel your dog's ribs before you ask him to go over jumps. Swimming is an excellent way to get your dog's weight down."

SUSAN'S TIP: "Most top agility competitors use a toy reward for their dog, especially a tug toy. Once you develop your dog's tug drive, you'll have a super-desirable reward with which to motivate him!"

IDEAL DOGS FOR THIS SPORT:

Height divisions separate dogs, so many breeds of dogs find success in agility. Border collies, Australian shepherds, and cattle dogs were bred to be quick and agile while herding animals—a characteristic that fares well in the sport of agility.

Border Collie "Nova" shows intense concentration as he one-steps through weave poles. Nova is owned by Animal Planet TV host Zak George.

Weave Pole Racing

Weave poles are one of the more difficult obstacles used in the sport of agility (page 12). They consist of straight line of upright poles through which the dog weaves in and out. In weave pole races (also called **slalom races**) dogs compete head-to-head in two identical sets of twenty-four, thirty-six, or more commonly sixty poles. The fastest dogs in the world will run through sixty poles in just under 10 seconds.

The dog must enter the set of weave poles with the first pole to his left. Handlers often position themselves to the right of the pole line, in order to help their dogs correctly make the entrance.

Dogs develop a rhythm as they bounce through the poles. Larger dogs will **sidestep** or **one-step** the poles. They step on just one front paw at a time, placing only one foot on each side of the pole line. Smaller dogs will **hop** through, placing both front paws together.

If a dog **pops a pole** (misses a pole), he must return to the missed pole and continue from there. Without a **clean run**, however, there is little chance of winning. Pole pops can happen when the dog tries to catch up to a handler who is ahead of him, which is why most handlers choose to run alongside their dog.

GEAR

Weave poles are about 3' (1 m) tall and spaced about 20"–24" (51–61 cm) apart. Make a backyard set by pounding pointed plastic PVC poles into your yard.

HOW TO GET STARTED

Use a short leash to guide your dog through a short set of poles, and give him a treat at the end.

MEET ALICIA NICHOLAS & PICKLE
60-WEAVE-POLE NATIONAL CHAMPION

"Pickle was a very good agility dog, and then he got a fungus called aspergillus and lost his left eye. After he recovered from his surgery we both had to retrain. I had to figure out how to best support him, such as by positioning myself on his 'eye side.' We did a ton of weave pole entry work (which was hard for Pickle because the first pole is always on his left, where he can't see it).

"The fact that he weaves again is incredible, but when he won the sixty-weave-pole challenge at the Purina Incredible Dog Challenge, I cried!"

ALICIA'S TIP: "Stay even with your dog, and don't go ahead of him. Encourage him all the way to the end."

IDEAL DOGS FOR THIS SPORT:

Larger dogs can have an advantage, which is why classes are sometimes divided by height. Border collies and herding breeds tend to dominate this event, but Shetland sheepdogs, terriers, and Doberman pinschers excel as well.

Border collie "Cayenne" does a swimmer's turn as he grabs his ball and heads back to the finish line.

Flyball

Flyball is a relay race between two teams, with four dogs on a team. Teams race head-to-head in identical, adjacent lanes which are 51' (15.5 m) long, with four hurdles placed 10' (3 m) apart. Each dog runs over the hurdles and jumps against a slanted **flyball box** at the end, releasing a spring-loaded tennis ball. With the ball in his mouth, he races back down the line of hurdles, crossing the start line to release the next dog on his team, until all four dogs have had their turn. The returning dog and the next dog will ideally cross the start line nose-to-nose (judged by an **Electronic Judging System**). At the elite level, dogs are released up to 40' (12 m) behind the start line so that they are running at full speed when they pass at the start line. Penalties are applied for an early release or a dropped ball. Handlers must remain behind the start line at all times.

Teams are seeded into divisions with other teams of similar speed, and each team races all the teams in his division. Teams that better their anticipated time by 1 second or more are said to **break out** of their division and consequently score no points (the break-out rule is intended to encourage teams to seed themselves accurately).

GEAR

Flyball boxes can have one, two, or three holes for the ball. Each dog will naturally prefer to turn to either his right or his left, and the ball is placed off-center to accommodate this. Tennis balls are standard, but squash balls are used for smaller dogs.

HOW TO GET STARTED

1. First, teach your dog to fetch a ball (page 97). Toss the ball toward the flybox and have him "fetch."

2. Next, put the ball in the flybox hole and send your dog to fetch. Send him with a lot of energy so he will hopefully jump on the box and trigger the ball's release. If he doesn't trigger the ball, encourage him to scratch at the box and figure out how to get the ball. See the following pages for more instruction.

MEET PAM MARTIN & PILOT WORLD CHAMPION RACING TEAM

"More than ever, specific breeds are being sought to perform in a chosen sport. Pilot is a borderjack (border collie, Jack Russell terrier cross). He is the height dog for our flyball 'A' team, which means he has to race every heat and be in top physical condition. His best asset is his ability to focus, which makes him easy to train. Pilot loves to run full out and race head-to-head with other dogs.

"After a competition, my thoughts are of the 'what if's...' 'if only we had...' and 'next time...'. Before I reach home I'm already planning out our next event! Life is short and Pilot and I will not always be together, so we plan to indulge whenever and where ever we can!"

PAM'S TIP: "Flyball is based on dogs who love balls, so having a good retrieve is really important."

IDEAL DOGS FOR THIS SPORT:

Herding breeds, Jack Russell terriers, and whippets currently dominate this sport. The flyball world record of just under 15 seconds was set by four border collie/American Staffordshire terrier mixes. The hurdle height for a team is determined by its smallest dog, varying from 7"–14" (18–36 cm), so one small dog per team is desirable.

Give your dog a head start in flyball by teaching him how to correctly retrieve the ball and return it over a line of hurdles.

BALL RETRIEVE:

See the instructions on page 97 to teach your dog to retrieve a ball from the flyball box.

There are two ways a dog can hit the flyball box and make a U-turn to head back. He can hit it straight on, known as a **slammer's turn**. But the preferred method is a **swimmer's turn** where the dog's front paws hit the box as the he gets the ball, and then his back legs push off the box in a turn, all in one fluid motion. A swimmer's turn is safe and fast.

1 Teach a swimmer's turn by first teaching your dog to run away from you, loop around a traffic cone, and run back.

2 Move the cone closer and closer to the flyball box, so your dog eventually has to run up on the box to get around the cone. Repeat this many times so that it becomes muscle memory for your dog.

3 Now it's time to add a jump before the flybox. We use a method called **backchaining**. The dog already knows the goal behavior (to get the ball and bring it back to you), and we will now start to add additional behaviors (hurdles) before the goal behavior. Stand at the start line and put a low hurdle in the path between your dog and the flyball box. This can be taught in a narrow hallway, so that your dog cannot go around the hurdle. Send your dog to "fetch" and reward him when he returns with the ball.

4 Add a second hurdle. Again, stand at the start line and send your dog to "fetch."

WHAT TO EXPECT: Dogs with a strong ball drive (dogs who love to play ball) can pick up this sport relatively quickly.

TIP: Remember to reward your dog for his retrieve; either with a toy, game of tug, or with a food treat.

1 Teach your dog to circle around a cone or pole.

2 Gradually scoot the cone closer to the flyball box. Your dog will have to bank a turn on the box to get around the cone.

3 Put a hurdle in your dog's path that he must jump over . . .

before he can achieve his goal behavior (fetching the ball).

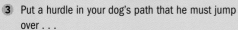

4 Add additional hurdles for your dog to traverse on his way to achieving the goal behavior.

OVERVIEW

In this challenging variation of flyball, agility obstacles are included in the race course.

A Nova Scotia duck-tolling retriever catches a ball launched from the flybox during a competition in New Zealand.

Flygility

This hybrid sport combines **flyball** (page 16) and **agility** (page 12) in a test of speed and teamwork. As in flyball, dogs run down and back a course, retrieving a ball from a flybox at the end. The 98' (30 m) course, however, contains agility obstacles. The handler stands behind the start line and directs his dog through the course. Three dogs form a team. Beginner-level competition courses consist of a straight line of jumps and tunnels and a flybox. Advanced courses are truly challenging, with U tunnels, weave poles, and changes of direction. If a dog is not successful on his run, he goes to the end of the line on his team and takes another turn. On his second turn, the handler runs alongside the dog. Flygility originated and still exists primarily in New Zealand and Australia.

GEAR

Different from flyball, the flygility **flybox** has a pedal that the dog steps on which lofts a ball from the back of the box toward the dog.

MEET KEVIN CROSSLEY & TASHI
NORTH SHORE DOG TRAINING CLUB, GREENHITHE, NEW ZEALAND

"My Australian shepherd, Tashi, was a natural at agility, but my injured knee was slowing us down. In flygility Tashi can run as fast as she wants, while I encourage her over the obstacles from the start/finish line."

KEVIN'S TIP: "Keep the exit area clear for the dog to cross into. Often a returning dog is reluctant to cross by another dog at the start/finish line who might be a threat."

OVERVIEW

Similar to flyball, dogs relay race over a line of hurdles. Dogs combine speed with mental concentration by picking out the one dumbbell holding their owner's scent.

Ten-year-old Shetland sheepdog "Nickles" competes on the Due South scent hurdle team at the Lethbridge & District Dog Show.

Scent Hurdle Racing

Scent hurdling was a precursor to **flyball** (page 16), but it is now a much less practiced sport. As in flyball, the dogs jump over a line of four hurdles. Instead of retrieving a ball at the end, the dog must find and retrieve the one dumbbell in four that has his owner's scent. This requires intense mental concentration.

Four numbered **scent articles**, each scented by one of the owners, are placed within a divided square platform. Each time a dumbbell is retrieved, the steward places an *X* (unscented dumbbell) on the empty space on the platform.

GEAR

Dogs wear a numbered jacket matching the number on their dumbbell (making it easier for the audience to see if the dog is returning with the correct dumbbell).

MEET JUDI SNOWDON & ROSE
DUE SOUTH SCENT HURDLE TEAM, ALBERTA CANADA

"I started in scent hurdling to add speed to my utility obedience scent discrimination exercise—and I got hooked on it!"

JUDI'S TIP: "Teach the routine in parts and then backchain the series. Start by teaching your dog to run back over the hurdles to the finish line. Then lay down one dumbbell and have him pick it up and run back over the hurdles. Then have him find the correct dumbbell out of several and run back over the hurdles. And finally have him run out, find the correct dumbbell, and run back."

Whippets "Dusty" (in pink) and
"Nola" (in yellow) chase after a lure
tied to a line at a coursing trial in
Florence, Texas.

Lure Coursing

Sighthounds rely on their sight, speed, and agility to hunt (unlike scent hounds, which rely on their noses and their endurance). A lure coursing race utilizes these inbred sighthound abilities by having them chase a mechanically operated artificial lure.

A typical lure course is between 600 and 1000 yards (549 and 914 m) long, and sometimes incorporate obstacles or jumps. The course has several turns that simulate the live coursing of a hare being chased. A **lure focused** dog will typically follow the lure from start to finish without running off course (although dogs with considerable lure experience may try to anticipate and cut off the lure). The lure is usually a small white garbage bag, although tanned rabbit skins or fake fur strips are also used. The lure is attached to a string that is pulled by a motor around the course, with pulleys to create turns. The lure travels at speeds up to 40 miles (64 km) per hour.

Dogs are coursed together by breed in **braces** (two dogs) or **trios** (three dogs). Each dog runs twice during the trial, the second run in the reverse direction from the first. When the race begins, the lure is started and the huntmaster cries "**Tally-Ho!**" to signal the release of the hounds. Dogs are judged on speed, agility, endurance, enthusiasm, and follow (pursuit of the lure.)

GEAR

The hounds wear brightly colored **coursing blankets**, usually pink, yellow, or cyan to identify them for scoring. For safety reasons, dogs are run without collars. A **slip lead** is used to control the hound prior to release. This consists of a broad, open-ended collar with a metal ring on each end. A leash is strung through the metal rings. When the owner releases one end of the leash, the collar and leash fall away.

HOW TO GET STARTED

Sighthounds an instinctual desire to chase the lure, and trainers encourage this drive by engaging the dog at an early age in lure play by wiggling a fake fur toy for him to chase and catch.

MEET ROBERT NEWMAN & PHOREST
#1 LURE COURSING PHARAOH HOUND

"Pharaoh hounds are sighthounds that were originally bred to hunt rabbits. I wanted my dogs to have the opportunity to do what they were born to do—run. To not allow them to run would be to not allow a bird to fly or a fish to swim."

"When Phorest was a puppy, I played with him with a lure whip, which is a whip with a fake rabbit pelt on the end for the dog to chase. Phorest, like most pharaoh hounds, has a naturally high prey drive, so I used the lure whip to develop and focus that natural drive."

ROBERT'S TIP: "Due to the strenuous nature of the sport, coursing dogs have to be in very good condition, or they will run an increased risk of injury. I keep Phorest in shape by regular walking and jogging and keeping an eye on his weight (more than I can do for myself!)."

IDEAL DOGS FOR THIS SPORT:

Only sighthounds may compete in sanctioned competition. Some sighthound breeds include: greyhound, Italian greyhound, whippet, saluki, Afghan hound, borzoi (Russian wolfhound), Irish wolfhound, Scottish deerhound, sloughi, basenji, Ibizan hound, pharaoh hound, and Rhodesian ridgeback.

OVERVIEW

Terriers sprint down a track, chasing after an artificial lure that ducks through a small hole at the finish line.

Jack Russell terriers leap over a hurdle in hot pursuit of a lure. Colored racing collars are used to identify the dogs and determine the order of finish. The dogs are muzzled for safety (theirs as well as the catchers).

Terrier Hurdle Racing

Dogs sprint down a 150'–200' (46–61 m) straight track chasing a **lure** (usually a piece of scented fur). The lure is attached to a string that is reeled in by a motor toward the finish line. The track has a starting box at one end and a stack of hay bales with a hole in the middle at the finish. The first dog to come through the hole in the hay bales is the winner. At the exit is a **catch pen** with catchers waiting to pick up the dogs. There are divisions according to age, height, and sometimes gender. There are two types of races: **flat** and **hurdles** (also known as **steeplechase**).

HOW TO GET STARTED

Tie a piece of fur (or a sock) to a 20' (6 m) string. Tease your dog with it and then run away, trailing the lure behind you. Let your dog catch the fur so it will be a satisfying experience for her.

MEET BONITA KNICKMEYER & KARMA
RACING CHAMPION

"If your dog is in a big class, and does well, it can be a long day: quarter-finals, semi-finals, and then finals. I don't know about my dog, but I come home exhausted!"

IDEAL DOGS FOR THIS SPORT:

Terriers breeds and dachshunds are allowed to compete, including Jack Russell terrier, fox terrier, border terrier, cairn terrier, miniature schnauzer, Norfolk terrier, and more.

Dachshunds approach the finish line during the Wienerschnitzel Wiener Nationals. Nearly 100 "wiener dogs" race at this event.

Wiener Dog Racing

Dachshund races (or wiener dog races) are hosted at race tracks as fundraising or publicity events and routinely draw the venues' largest attendance numbers of the year. *Wiener Takes All* was a dogumentary comic look at this tongue-in-cheek sport that was first introduced as a parody in a beer commercial.

Typical wiener races are either 25 or 50 yards (23 or 46 m) in length. Most events are informal, with pet dogs who are not career racers. Often, dogs will choose not to run the length of the course and instead visit with other dogs or the owner that released them. Other dogs will run swiftly to their owner at the finish line, coaxed by food or toys.

The **Wienerschnitzel Wiener Nationals** is considered the "national championships" of the sport and draws a crowd of 10,000.

MEET HALEY HARLAND & MAX
WIENERSCHNITZEL WIENER RACE CHAMPION

"Max beat out 85 dachshund competitors at the nationals to earn the title of 'Fastest Wiener in the West,' with a time of 7 seconds for the 50-yard (46 m) race.

"Wiener dog racing is a charity event. With dachshunds' long backs, they are not built for hard running."

HALEY'S TIP: "The dachsies can get pretty excited at the start of the race, so it can be hard to keep them focused. Bring your dog's favorite toy or food treat and run with it toward the finish line."

OVERVIEW

Trail hounds follow a
cross-country course of
approximately 10 miles
(16 km) marked by a
scent trail. This race is
regulated and is a form
of gambling.

Trailhounds tear across the
Cumbrian landscape competing
in the Lazonby Hound Trail.

Hound Trailing

In this traditional Cumbrian sport, hounds race over the fells following a scented trail in a test of speed and stamina. The artificial **scent trail** is laid by **trailers** who drag a scented rag across the course. Two trailers meet at the halfway point and then walk away from each other, one laying the trail to the start and one laying the trail to the finish.

Owners and supporters gather at the start of the trail, often along with stalls for bets to be placed on the winning dog and stands selling food and drink. The dogs are lined up and held by their owners. At the starting gun they are slipped to follow the course, which covers difficult terrain similar to steeplechasing, wherein the dogs jump over obstacles such as fences. The trail hounds can average speeds of 20 miles (32 km) per hour. The hounds are not encouraged to hunt as a pack, as they do in **drag hunting** (page 94), but rather to race as individuals. The best dogs ignore distractions, such as rabbit scents, to cover the 10 miles (16 km) in 25 to 45 minutes.

When the hounds come into sight the owners wave their dog food buckets and shout to their own hounds, each owner having her own noise and each hound knowing the noise that belongs to him. Judging at the finish line is often a close call, with a "photo finish" sometimes used to decide the result. Winning dogs collect points toward the coveted title of champion.

GEAR

The scent the dogs follow is made from aniseed (which is a strong scent) to which paraffin is added as a fixative so that the scent doesn't evaporate.

HOW TO GET STARTED

Hound trailing originated in Cumbria, England, and is practiced primarily in northern England and Ireland. Scent trailing is an instinctual drive in hounds, and they do not require much training. Often a novice hound is paired with an experienced hound during training.

Teach your dog to track a short distance by dragging a scent through wet grass (which holds scent well). Leave a treat at the end of the trail to encourage your dog to follow the scent. Read more about teaching your dog to track on pages 84–85.

MEET DEBBIE O'BRIEN & TARMAC DAVE & BANDIT
CUMBRIA, ENGLAND

"I love trail because we all go as a family. My daughters (ages 6 and 7) each have a hound, so this year we will be running all four dogs. Our hounds are part of our family and are very loving and soft natured at home.

"Trailhounds love to race. We have dog hounds [males] and I can hardly lead them to the start of a race as they get so strong (I have been pulled off my feet several times!). There is tremendous noise and excitement at the start of the race. Seeing my hounds lead in a race is brilliant. Often they are overtaken before the finish, but it is just a nice feeling to know that they have done their best and have tried for me."

DEBBIE'S TIP: "Our first trailhound was an older, experienced hound that was given to us, and her previous owners gave us a lot of helpful advice."

IDEAL DOGS FOR THIS SPORT:

Foxhounds were originally used for this sport, but through selective breeding leaner-build trailhounds are now used because they are faster and have a good nose. There are various classes of competition including puppies, maidens, seniors, and veterans.

OVERVIEW

Based on historic "war dog" duties, dogs speedily carry messages back and forth between two people.

Belgian Tervuren "Apollo" carries his results slip in a container on his collar.

Alsatian (German shepherd dog) "Allt-I" competes in a messenger dog trial in Sweden. She is required to wear a Svenska Brukshundklubben working dog cape when training or competing.

Messenger Dog

Messenger dog trials (also known as **rapporthund**) is a form of canine competition based on military dogs who were once used to deliver messages on the battlefield quickly, quietly, and unnoticed. This tough discipline requires mental balance, courage, speed, agility, strength, and endurance.

Messenger dog competition is a team sport consisting of a dog and two handlers. The dog runs a relatively long distance between the two handlers to "deliver a message" (carried on her collar). Ideally, the dog is equally bonded to both handlers (often handlers are a husband and a wife or a parent and child). The dog must achieve the distance within a set time and must do so without barking, whining, or making excessive noise.

Competition messenger dog trials are held primarily in Scandinavia, especially in Sweden. In novice competition the dog must traverse 1 km (2 legs of 500 m) within 7 minutes combined time (the clock is suspended at each stopping point). In expert competition, she must traverse 6.1 km (comprised of legs of 1100 + 1500 + 1500 + 2000 m) within 36 minutes. (The fastest dogs achieve this between 13 to 17 minutes, depending on terrain). This distance is comprised of several trips back and forth between two handlers. One handler is stationary, and the other walks farther away with each trip so the dog must track his scent to find him. In scoring, the fastest dog gets 290 points, and for every 90 seconds slower than the fastest time, 14.5 points are deducted.

GEAR

Messenger dogs wear a working dog harness. Upon reaching the handler, a white flag is sometimes tied to the dog's harness so that the judge can be sure that the dog did indeed reach his mark (although phones are more commonly used today). The dog wears a container on her collar that holds the dog's result slip upon which the judge writes the times of each leg of her trip.

HOW TO GET STARTED

Practice in the woods, by having your dog run between her two owners. Each owner should praise the dog heartily and give her treats when she arrives.

MEET INGRID BAHLENBERG & ALLT-I MESSENGER DOG CHAMPION AND JUDGE, ESKILSTUNA, SWEDEN

"I am athletic myself, and I like to keep my dog physically fit as well. Not only is rapporthund great exercise, but my husband and I enjoy having a sport where we can train and compete together as a team.

"My dog Allt-I has won many titles. Allt-I is Swedish and means 'she's got what it takes.'"

INGRID'S TIP: "Rapporthund is very much about recollection training. Start with very short distances and short waiting times to set your dog up for success. Anytime your dog fails, you know that you have increased the distance and duration too quickly. Give your dog lots of encouragement and rewards in order to get the fastest run."

IDEAL DOGS FOR THIS SPORT:

German shepherd dogs, Bouvier des Flandres, and Airedale terriers are traditional message carriers, but Tervuren, Belgian sheepdogs, and similar breeds are also often seen in competition. The dog must be physically fit, have good endurance, and be motivated to run alone in the woods without being distracted.

Brindle greyhound "Soaring Cindy" holds the high jump world record of 5' 8" (173 cm).

High Jump

High-jump events take place at dog challenge competitions. Commonly, two people will handle the dog. One holds the dog while the other motivates the dog with a disc or favorite toy on the other side of the jump.

GEAR

Set up a bar jump or create a homemade version with two chairs and a broomstick. For safety reasons, the bar should easily release if hit.

HOW TO GET STARTED

Work on a surface that provides good traction and a soft landing for your dog.

1. Set the bar to a low height: 3"–6" (8–15 cm) for small dogs and 12"–18" (31–46 cm) for medium-size dogs. With your dog on a lead, run with him toward the jump. Give an enthusiastic "hup!" as you jump over the bar with him and praise him for his success. A treat may be given; however, most dog enjoy the jump on its own. If your dog is reluctant, lower the bar to the ground and walk over it with him. Avoid pulling him over the jump and give him plenty of encouragement.

2. As your dog's confidence improves, gradually raise the bar and run alongside the jump, rather than over it.

3. Now try it off leash. It can sometimes help to toss a toy over the jump.

Most dogs enjoy jumping and will take to it easily if given positive feedback. Within a few days, your dog can be a jumper!

IDEAL DOGS FOR THIS SPORT:

Tall, lightweight dogs are ideal. These include greyhound, Afghan hound, saluki, borzoi, Irish wolfhound, and Scottish deerhound. Other less tall dogs with a lean, athletic build include Weimaraner, vizsla, pointer, German shorthaired pointer, and Doberman. Herding dogs have incredible drive, and some are able to clear surprisingly high jumps: border collie, Australian shepherd, collie, German shepherd dog, and Belgian Malinois.

Three-year-old yellow Labrador retriever "Cruiser" does a warm-up jump before the competes at the Purina Incredible Dog Challenge East Coast Finals. Cruiser easily clears three jumps for a distance of 10 feet (3 m), peaking at 40" (1 m) high.

Long Jump

Canine long jump (or **broad jump**) is an exhibition sport and therefore varies in its standards. Top dogs will clear a 9' (2.7 m) distance over a height of 24" (61 cm). The dog needs about 20' (6 m) of runway in front of the jump. One trainer releases the dog from the start, and another trainer waves a disc or toy at the far end of the jump and calls to the dog.

GEAR

Obedience and agility competitions incorporate a broad jump obstacle made of four slightly raised, slanted planks. In extreme long jump competitions, however, the distances are much longer, and therefore one or several bar jumps are added (sometimes above the planks) to really encourage the arc of the dog's jump. Bar jumps are distributed equidistant, approximately 24" (61 cm) apart.

MEET LOURDES EDLIN & CRUISER
COMPETITORS

"I use the broad jump to warm up and build strength for dock diving. Cruiser (like most Labs) loves to play. I wave his favorite ball or Frisbee on the far side of the jump to motivate him."

IDEAL DOGS FOR THIS SPORT:

Tall, lightweight dogs such as the greyhound and borzoi excel at long jump. Successful dock diving (page 72) dogs can often be successful at the long jump as well.

TEACH IT:

A dog can execute a jump using a variety of arcs and body positions. For this sport, we want to teach the dog to elongate his jump by elongating his arc and his body position. Notice how "Cruiser" in the photo left is stretched almost flat, and notice how "Thunder" below becomes more elongated as he extends his jump.

First, teach your dog to jump over a low bar jump (page 31). Mark a start line and bring your dog to that line to start every jump.

1 Set a bar jump to a low height and add two broad jump planks very near to the base of the jump.

2 Add a second bar jump. If your dog is familiar with the sport of agility (page 12) he may think he is supposed to touch ground between each jump. We extend broad jump planks between the two jumps to cue the dog that this is all one obstacle, to be jumped in a single leap.

3 Gradually widen the distance between the jumps and the planks.

TIP: Your job as coach is to provide a consistent and motivating environment for your dog's jumps. Measure everything, including the distance of your dog's starting runway.

1 Teach your dog to jump over a bar jump.

2 Add a second bar jump and additional planks.

3 Gradually widen the distances, making sure to measure and set jumps consistently.

OVERVIEW

Teach your dog to jump through a hoop for a fun game and easy exercise.

Alaskan malamute "Kwest" jumps through a hoop.

Hoop Jumping

Hoop jumping is not a competitive sport, but rather a skill that can be used to exercise your dog or as an element in a dog dancing or stunt dog routine. A hoop jump is similar to the tire jump obstacle used in the sport of agility (page 12).

GEAR

Remove any noisy beads from within the hoop as the sound may frighten your dog.

HOW TO GET STARTED

Allow your dog time to investigate the hoop and overcome any fear she has of it. It is important that you allow your dog to make the decision to go through the hoop on her own, without forcing her.

1. Hold the hoop on the ground, touching the wall with one edge to prevent your dog from going around the hoop instead of through it. Hold the hoop with the hand closest to your dog. Use your other hand to lure your dog through with a treat. Let her have the treat once she walks through.

2. As your dog gets the idea, begin to raise the hoop off the floor. Dogs sometimes get tangled in the hoop, so be prepared to release it if you feel resistance.

3. Assuming your dog has the physical ability, raise the hoop again so that your dog must jump to get through it. Try giving her a running start or use your hand on the opposite side of the hoop to lure her upward.

Dogs usually get the hang of hoop jumping within a week or two and do it enthusiastically.

MEET LANA MAEDER & DIVA
HOOP DANCERS

"I'm a hoop dancer myself, so it seemed obvious to incorporate that prop into my trick dog show. I developed a routine with Diva which is dog dancing—but with hoops. I'll swing the hoop on my own body and then do some spin moves where Diva jumps through it. I love the options it gives me to be more creative with our show!"

LANA'S TIP: "See how many moves you can come up with using a hoop!"

IDEAL DOGS FOR THIS ACTIVITY:

All dogs can benefit from the exercise that hoop jumping provides. Young dogs seem to show the most joy for jumping back and forth over and over.

1

2

3

OVERVIEW

Get fit along with your dog as you jump rope together!

Kyra Sundance and her Weimaraner "Chalcy" cohosted the televised "Worldwide Fido Awards," where they perform a variety of tricks such as jumping rope.

Rope Jumping

There are a variety of ways to work with this noncompetitive sport. You can jump rope with your dog; you can tie off one end of the rope and swing the other end while your dog jumps in the middle; or two people can swing the ends of the rope while your dog jumps.

GEAR

Use a flexible rope that is approximately 9' (2.7 m) long and ⅞" (2 cm) thick.

HOW TO GET STARTED

This sport can take dogs months or longer to master. Practice in short sessions and keep up the enthusiasm. Here's how to start teaching your dog to jump with you.

1. While your dog is in a playful mood, encourage him to jump by holding a toy or food in the air and teasing him with it. Reward even small jumps by giving him the treat or toy.

2. Next, try it without the toy. Say a lively "hup!" and jump to encourage your dog. Hold the rope in your hand to start to get your dog used to it.

3. Gently accustom your dog to the rope. Hold the rope behind your dog and let it fall lightly behind him. After the rope falls, cue your dog to "hup!" and reward him for jumping (even though he is not jumping over the rope at this point).

4. It will take time for your dog to learn the rhythm of the rope and the timing of your cue. Reward your dog for jumping, even if he doesn't clear the rope.

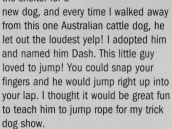

MEET TRISH PERONDI & DASH
TRICK DOG SHOW PERFORMERS

"I was searching the shelter for a new dog, and every time I walked away from this one Australian cattle dog, he let out the loudest yelp! I adopted him and named him Dash. This little guy loved to jump! You could snap your fingers and he would jump right up into your lap. I thought it would be great fun to teach him to jump rope for my trick dog show.

"First I taught Dash to jump in place, and then I tried to add the rope. That's when I learned that Dash was afraid of the rope. Using a clicker I was able to acclimate him to the rope in a positive way—it's all about positive reinforcement! Today he is the star of our show!"

TRISH'S TIP: "Things don't happen overnight. Have a goal for each training session of just getting results a little better than the last time."

IDEAL DOGS FOR THIS ACTIVITY:

"Bouncy" dogs will work best for this activity: Jack Russell terriers, fox terriers, miniature Australian shepherds, West Highland white terriers, and even American Staffordshire terriers.

OVERVIEW

Hold a baton in a variety of positions for your dog to jump over. Get creative!

One-year-old Weimaraner "Jadie" loves to baton jump and will do so just for fun—even without treats!

Baton Jumping

In baton jumping (also called **stick jumping**), your dog jumps over a handheld baton. You can position the baton horizontally in a variety of ways: to your side, on your knee, or above your head as you crouch down. This can be used to exercise your dog, and by changing the position that you hold the baton with every jump, it can be good exercise for you as well.

GEAR

Make a simple baton with a wooden dowel or broomstick. Professional batons are available through cheerleading catalogs and are properly weighted to allow them to move and spin easily in your hands.

HOW TO GET STARTED

1. Warm up with your dog jumping over a bar (page 31). Stand alongside the jump and use a sweeping motion with the arm farthest from your dog to signal him over.

2. Remove the jump and hold just the bar parallel to the ground using the arm closest to your dog. Cue him to "hup" and lure him over with a treat in your other hand. If your dog tries to go around the bar, hold the other end against a wall.

Experiment with changing your body positions after every jump in a sequence of jumps. Your dog can learn the basics of baton jumping in a few weeks, however, every new body position will require a learning period as you and your dog figure out the logistics. This collaborative effort is a true bonding experience.

KYRA SUNDANCE & CHALCY
STUNT DOG TEAM

"I love baton jumping because I can just throw a baton in my bag and give an impromptu show wherever I am. I taught myself some basic twirling moves so that in between jumps I can do a flashy twirl or even toss the baton in the air and catch it again.

"One of my favorite moves is a somersault. I crouch down and hold the baton just over my head. As soon as my dog jumps over me, I roll forward. When we do it fast it looks like a continuous motion."

KYRA'S TIP: "A real twirler's baton is a lot easier to use than a wooden dowel or other stick. It moves back and forth in your hands without falling (as much)."

IDEAL DOGS FOR THIS ACTIVITY:

Breeds that jump high will allow you more creativity in your body positions when you hold the baton. There are many breeds that meet this qualification, such as greyhound, Jack Russell terrier, whippet, Belgian Malinois, dalmatian, and golden retriever.

Dogrobatics creator Kyra Sundance and her Weimaraners performed their synchronized tumbling show on *The Tonight Show* and in the palace of the King of Morocco. In these photos Kyra demonstrates a "swan" jump (above) and a "matrix" jump (right).

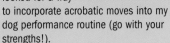

Dogrobatics

In this athletic exhibition sport, dog and handler perform choreographed synchronized acrobatics and energetic tumbling maneuvers such as the dog jumping over the handler's back, over parts of her body, or through her legs while she does a handstand. Hoops and batons may be incorporated. Dogrobatics shows are performed at professional sports halftime shows and as exhibitions on television and at corporate events.

The basis of dogrobatics is the handler staying in the same spot while the dog runs back and forth executing jumps over the handler with each pass. The dog is taught to run back and forth between two **targets** (such as cones) that are placed 24' (7.3 m) apart. The targets are necessary for two reasons. Firstly, they are necessary to get the dog far enough away from the handler so that the dog can get enough running speed for a high jump and so that the handler has enough time between jumps to change her body position. And secondly, targets are necessary because they facilitate the dog landing straight and not twisting in mid-air in an attempt to curve back to her handler.

Positioning four targets in a square configuration (see photos below) allows the handler to send her dog diagonally between cones in a variety of ways.

GEAR

When selecting a target cone, be aware that dogs' vision is color limited, and orange cones on green grass will not stand out well.

HOW TO GET STARTED

Teach your dog the basics by teaching him to jump over a baton (page 39) and to touch a target (page 154). Practice sending him back and forth between two target cones, and jumping a bar or baton with each pass.

KYRA SUNDANCE
SUNDANCE DOG TEAM

"I have a background in gymnastics, so I looked for a way to incorporate acrobatic moves into my dog performance routine (go with your strengths!).

"Initially I set up with just two target cones, and my dog would run back and forth between the two. When I started performing at halftime shows, I suddenly had an audience 360° around me, so I started experimenting with setting up a second set of two cones. Hmm ... that looks a lot like a square!"

KYRA'S TIP: "Synchronization is key in this sport. Keep your eye on your dog until she has committed to the jump. Turn your head in the direction of the body part you wish your dog to jump as a cue for her. Develop sequences of three or four moves, and always practice them as a sequence."

IDEAL DOGS FOR THIS ACTIVITY:

Many of the acrobatic moves involve the dog jumping over your entire body, so the dog needs to have jump height. Weimaraners, greyhounds, standard poodles, and Great Danes are good choices, as are any dogs with high energy and athletic bodies.

OVERVIEW

A team of dogs pulls a sled over the snow, taking direction from the driver.

A team of Siberian and Alaskan huskies goes on an early morning training run on a graded trail in Alaska.

Sled Dog Racing

Dogs can earn sled dog titles through competitive races or by completing a set number of runs of a minimum distance. The **Iditarod Trail Sled Dog Race** in Alaska is the most challenging and competitive sled dog race in the world, covering over a thousand miles (1,609 km).

GEAR

Dogs wear X-back harnesses and travel two-by-two, attached to a gangline. Dog boots are used to protect a dog's foot pads when ice is sharp and granular or when the team is traveling a long distance.

HOW TO GET STARTED

The sled dogs' strong **pull drive** comes out when the dogs are part of a team or when other dogs are pulling sleds around them. Train with another sled dog team to test your dog's drive. Dogs get competitive and sometimes try to bite at each other—keep aware!

MEET SAM DELTOUR
IDITAROD RACER, SINT-KRUIS, BELGIUM

"Racing the Iditarod makes me humble. Dogs function as a mirror for our emotions, character, and weaknesses. My mistakes will be reflected by my dogs."

SAM'S TIP: "No matter how tired you are, or how cold, or thirsty, or hungry, the dogs come first. The dogs always come first. They need to trust you to take care of their needs."

IDEAL DOGS FOR THIS SPORT:

Alaskan malamutes and Siberian huskies are adapted to cold weather with tough feet and have endurance and a desire to run. Seppala Siberian sleddogs, Japanese akitas, and crossbreeds are also common.

OVERVIEW

Similar to sled dog racing, land mushing is done on dirt with a wheeled cart instead of a sled.

Alaskan malamute "Kwest" leads the team of Korean jindos, akitas, and malamutes through the California's Mojave desert.

Land Mushing

Mushing is a term for dog-powered transportation, thought to originate from the French *marcher,* meaning to go or run. In land mushing, the driver stands on the metal skids of a three-wheeled land cart.

Mushing commands are "**gee**" (pronounced JEE; turn right), "**haw**" (turn left), "**on by**" (bypass a road), "**hike!**" (go!), "**whoa**" (stop), and "**line out**" (lead dogs keep the line taut while stopped to prevent tangling). **Lead dogs** are at the front of the team, followed by **swing dogs**, which swing the team on curves; **team dogs** are in the middle, with **wheel dogs** closest to the sled or cart.

GEAR

Pack water, bowls, a first-aid kit, and a GPS. Care for your dog's foot pads with appropriate topical treatments.

MEET NICHOLE ROYER & KWEST

"After adopting a Korean jindo and an Alaskan malamute, I went to a mushing clinic, where I drove a big team of working line Siberians—it was life changing. I scraped together the money to buy a cart and adopted an older Siberian husky who was a trained gee/haw leader dog but no longer fast enough to race. 'Dee' led my team until she was 15 and taught us to be real mushers."

IDEAL DOGS FOR THIS SPORT:

Sporting breeds such as Eurohounds and German shorthaired pointers are fast, athletic, large enough to pull, and often have a strong pull drive.

OVERVIEW

This accessible sport is easy to learn and provides exercise for both you and your dog.

Kyra Sundance and her Weimaraner "Chalcy" mush through California's Mojave Desert.

Scootering

One to three dogs pull a driver riding an unmotorized scooter (also called **kick bike**), which has mountain-bike-style brakes and a large footboard to kick off from. The dogs wear the same harnesses that sled dogs wear and are hooked to the scooter with a **tugline** which incorporates a **shockline** (a bungee cord to smooth out the speed).

GEAR

Rugged dog scooters are designed to be stable on rough terrain. A **brushbow** attachment or foam noodle can be used to keep the line from going under the wheel. A helmet and gloves are a good idea.

HOW TO GET STARTED

See instructions on pages 46–47 to get started in this sport.

MEET LAURA MITOBE & MAESTRO

"After many years of being very overweight, I lost over 100 pounds (45 kg). I knew the key to keeping the weight off was to stay active, so I took up dog scootering. Finishing a long, challenging run is exhilarating and gives me the confidence to accomplish even more. The more I do with my dogs, the better I feel and the more physically fit I become."

IDEAL DOGS FOR THIS SPORT:

Scootering is usually a recreational rather than a competitive sport, so you'll see a wide variety of breeds participating. Dogs are generally over 35 pounds (16 kg).

Alaskan huskies bikejoring across the Yukon Territory in Canada.

Bikejoring

In bikejoring you ride a bicycle with your dog (or two dogs) pulling you. Bikejoring is primarily a vehicle for exercising your dog rather than gaining a workout for yourself. It is more dangerous than scootering because it is harder for the rider to dismount, should things go awry. Because there must always be tension the **towline** to avoid it getting tangled in the wheel, the rider feathers his brakes most of the time.

GEAR

Plastic pipes (or **bay-o-nets** or **antennas**) can be used to hold the towline over the tire, so that it doesn't get caught under it.

HOW TO GET STARTED

Dogs should have experience pulling in harness (scootering, sled dog, or canicross) before trying bikejoring.

MEET SARA VANDERWOOD
BIKEJORING CHAMPION

"For my 5th birthday I got Katrina, a Siberian husky, and we entered our first sled race. I was hooked! Many years later when my son was three months old, I put him in a pulk and entered a skijoring race (and we won!). I started bikejoring as a way to condition my dogs during the summer."

SARA'S TIP: "Bikejoring is a fast sport and you need to have quick reflexes!"

IDEAL DOGS FOR THIS SPORT:

Northern breeds are bred to pull, but American Staffordshire terriers, and sporting dogs are also popular.

Teach your dog to hold the line taut and pull in harness.

LINE OUT AND PULL:

Scootering and bikejoring require the following items: a scooter or bike with rugged tires, a dog harness, a tugline, and a neckline (used if you ride with more than one dog). You should wear protective gear such as a helmet, gloves, knee pads, and sunglasses or goggles (to protect from debris kicked up by your dogs.) Someone in your group should carry water, a first-aid kit, and navigational tools.

1. Put a well-fitting harness on your dog. Attach the tugline from your scooter to the ring on the back of the harness.

2. First, teach your dog to **line out**, or pull the line taut. Lay the scooter down and use a treat to lure your dog away from the scooter until he is slightly pulling in his harness. Tell him "good line out" and give him the treat. Next, see if you can get him to hold the line taut for a little longer before giving him the treat.

3. Stand the scooter upright and walk next to it as a friend walks next to or in front of your dog, encouraging him to pull. Praise your dog for pulling.

4. Ride on your scooter while your friend runs or rides a bike ahead or your dog, acting as a "rabbit" for your dog to chase. If your dog is not enthusiastic about chasing the person, have the person take a dog with them.

5. Gradually fade out "rabbit" by having the person disappear around a corner or off in the distance.

WHAT TO EXPECT: Most dogs respond to the "rabbit" training technique pretty easily and can be mushing on their first day. A dog will always be more enthusiastic to run when there are other mushing dogs that he can compete against. Get some friends together with their dogs and scooters to run as a group.

TIP: If at any time the line goes slack, lightly brake and encourage your dog to line out. Teach puppies this sport by allowing them to run along freely beside the adult dogs on training runs.

TUGLINE

SCOOTER

HARNESS

NECKLINE

1. Attach the tugline from your scooter to the back ring on your dog's harness.

2. Use a treat to lure your dog to the end of the tugline. Praise him and give him the treat.

Gradually lengthen the time your dog keeps the line taut before giving him the treat.

3. Walk next to the scooter as a friend walks ahead of your dog, encouraging him to pull.

4. Ride on your scooter as a friend acts as a "rabbit" for your dog to chase.

5. Have the "rabbit" disappear out of view, up ahead or around a corner.

Alaskan huskies pull a racer at Park City Mountain Resort in Utah.

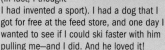

Skijoring

Skijor racing (derived from the Norwegian word skikjøring meaning ski driving) involves one to three dogs pulling a person on cross-country skis. The skijorer provides power with skis and poles, and the dog adds additional power by running and pulling.

The sport is practiced recreationally and competitively, both for long distance travel and for short (sprint) distances. Most skijor races are 5–20 km in length (3–12.4 miles) and are held in many countries where there is snow in winter. In some competitions races are separated into men's and women's and one-dog and two-dog categories.

In Scandinavia, skijor racing is tightly associated with the older Scandinavian sport of **pulka driving** that involves skijoring with a small sled (pulk) between skijorer and dog.

GEAR

A skijoring harness is a wide waistband that is clipped around the skijorer's waist and which may include leg loops to keep it in position. Rock climbing harnesses are also commonly used. The dog wears a sled dog harness (which must have a proper fit) and the two are connected by a 8–10' (2.4–3 m) **tugline**, which may have a quick-release.

HOW TO GET STARTED

The skier uses either a classic diagonal stride cross-country technique or the faster skate skiing technique. Initial training should be done on foot (see canicross, page 50), before the person straps on her skis.

MEET KIM TINKER & BA-REE
3X PACIFIC NORTHWEST CHAMPION

"I got into this sport by accident (in fact, I thought I had invented a sport). I had a dog that I got for free at the feed store, and one day I wanted to see if I could ski faster with him pulling me—and I did. And he loved it!"

"My feed store dog was named Ba-Ree (which means wolf dog.) He is a malamute/shepherd/wolf cross. Larger dogs like Ba-Ree aren't usually used for skijoring because they can't usually keep up speed for long distances, but Ba-Ree is different!"

"I now own six Alaskan husky skijor dogs. They are German shorthaired pointer/husky crosses, and several also have a little saluki mixed in."

KIM'S TIP: "Have some basic cross-country skiing skills before you start. And remember, there is no such thing as a hyper dog—only an exercise-dependent dog."

IDEAL DOGS FOR THIS SPORT:

Alaskan huskies and Eurohounds are ideal mushing dogs. Neither are an official breed but rather a loose description of a type of cross. The Alaskan husky is a northern breed dog averaging about 40–50 pounds (18–23 kg). The Eurohound is a sprinter, and is a cross between Alaskan husky and a hound or sporting dog such as a pointer.

Northern breeds such as Siberian huskies, malamutes, samoyeds, and Inuit dogs are naturals, as are pulling breeds such as American bull terriers, Staffordshire terriers, American bull dogs, and mastiffs. Any energetic and athletic dog can enjoy skijoring.

WAISTBAND

WAISTBAND WITH LEG LOOPS

OVERVIEW

In this variation of cross-country running, dogs assist the runner by pulling a tugline attached to his waist.

Siberian huskies "Alexi" and "Pascha" take their owner for a cross-country run outside the Crufts dog show in Birmingham, England.

Canicross / Caniteering

Originating in Europe as off-season training for the mushing (sledding) community, canicross has become a popular sport. Canicross can be run with one or two dogs, which are joined to the runner by a bungee cord (or **tugline**) that reduces shock to both human and dog when the dog pulls.

People of all ages and abilities can take part, including children and the visually impaired. Canicross is not only a great way for the runner to keep fit, but it's great for the dogs too. Canicross races cover distances from 1 km (0.6 miles) up to 45 km (28 miles) or more.

For a variation on canicross, try **caniteering**. Originally a training exercise in land navigation for military officers, **orienteering** involves a race using navigational skills to find marker points specified on a map. Racers must navigate from marker to marker in diverse and usually unfamiliar terrain. Caniteering is a fledgling sport that utilizes speed and navigation skills with your dog. Caniteering combines canicross with orienteering and provides dogs and owners with ample opportunities to get lost. Runners go off road and make their own paths, often through close wooded areas. A reward for your dog at each marker keeps them enthusiastic about the run!

GEAR

The dog wears a sledding harness and the runner wears a specially designed waist belt. In competitions there are more detailed requirements for the clips and the length of the line. A hydration pack provides water for both runner and dog.

HOW TO GET STARTED

Teach your dog to run in front of you, and not veer off the trail. Choose a running spot without many distractions, such as a sport track. If your dog veers off course or stops suddenly, use a cue word such as "go!" to startle him and get him back on track.

MEET SIMON LAMEN & SHANAY FOUNDER OF CANITEERING, WILTSHIRE, ENGLAND

"My wife and I have been canicrossing for over 14 years (although in the beginning, we didn't know our sport even had a name)! I am a competitive runner, and I used to enter races and then have to come home and still take my dogs for a run. One day I read about a canicross race—what a fabulous discovery! We took our Siberian huskies to our first race and met some lifelong friends.

"As a soldier in the British Army, I have orientated for many years. I had the idea of combining that with canicross into a new sport which I called caniteering."

SIMON'S TIP: "Time with your dog is rewarding and rejuvenating. I've solved many problems whilst running with my dogs. Its not just a walk—it is a cleansing workout for the mind."

IDEAL DOGS FOR THIS SPORT:

Some breeds are well suited to running and pulling at steady pace over a long distance. Originally canicross dogs were of sledding or spitz types such as the husky or malamute, but now all breeds have begun taking part including small terrier breeds and large breeds such as Rottweilers and standard poodles.

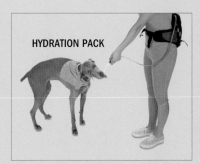

HYDRATION PACK

Bernese mountain dogs pull a hay
cart in Tervuren, Belgium.

OVERVIEW

Dogs were historically
used on farms to haul
carts of firewood,
produce, or milk. Today
dog carting is done
recreationaly and as a
titling sport.

Dog Carting

In dog carting (also called **draft dog**) a dog pulls a two-wheel cart or four-wheel wagon filled with supplies such as firewood or farm goods. Dog carts pulled by two or more dogs were historically used in Belgium and the Netherlands for delivering milk. Dog-drawn carts were prohibited in Britain in the early 1900s on animal welfare grounds, but some still exist (mainly for reasons of novelty) in France and Belgium for delivering churns of milk from small farms to the dairy. A variety of carting is **sulky driving**, where a dog or dogs pull a two-wheeled sulky with a human driver and is steered with reins similar to those used on horses.

For a dog to pull a weighted cart he must be physically conditioned. A 90 pound (41 kg) dog (or several smaller dogs) can pull an adult and a sulky comfortably. The rule of thumb is a dog can pull up to three times his weight with a wheeled vehicle.

Dog carting offers both exercise and discipline opportunities for energetic breeds. Many working breeds are happier when given a job or task, and carting can be a rewarding hobby for both dog and owner. Not only is dog carting a fun recreational hobby, but some breed and kennel clubs have sanctioned carting titles that a dog can earn.

GEAR

There are several styles of harness: **parade harness** (straps around the dog's chest and forechest), **Siwash harness** (similar to a sled dog harness), and **draft harness** (resembling the draft rigs normally seen on horses).

You'll need a cart or wagon and a **shaft** (rigid bars that connect from the wagon through loops on the sides of the dog's harness). Shafts steer the wagon. Leather strap **traces** hook into both sides of your dog's harness and are what the dog uses to pull.

HOW TO GET STARTED

Use the instructions on the following pages to introduce your dog to the equipment and teach him to pull a cart.

MEET TUBBY MILLER & LEXI
GOLD MEDAL WINNER, CARTING OLYMPICS

"When I was a kid in Winnipeg [Canada] my mom read a story to me of a Newfoundland rescuing a drowning girl, and I became fascinated with the breed. I have been carting with Newfies for over 35 years and have put 50 draft dog titles on my dogs.

"When I start, I spend 15–20 minutes a day getting the dog used to the cart and shafts. I was able to hook Lexi up to the cart in two days, but one of my dogs needed almost 6 months!

TUBBY'S TIP: "The most challenging part of teaching your dog will be transitioning from walking beside your dog, to walking behind the cart and driving the dog and cart."

IDEAL DOGS FOR THIS ACTIVITY:

Carting is generally done by large breed dogs. Several breeds of dogs have been specifically bred for this work, including the Rottweiler, Saint Bernard, Bernese mountain dog, greater Swiss mountain dog, Newfoundland, mastiff, Leonberger, and more. Those that were not bred for this purpose can be trained to do this kind of work. There are even very small harnesses carts designed for dogs as small as a papillon!

Train your dog to wear a harness and to pull a cart.

PULL A CART:

Gently outfit your dog in a carting harness. Most dogs are not bothered by a harness, but give her a little time to get used to it.

1 Attach the traces to the sides of your dog's harness and attach a leash to her collar. Walk her on a leash, letting her get used to the traces tickling her legs and sides.

2 Next, accustom your dog to the noise of the cart behind her. Don't attach the apparatus to your dog but rather walk beside your dog, holding the shaft in your hand. If your gets scared, simply lift up the shafts and your dog will be able to escape them.

3 Attach the shafts to your dog's harness. Attach a leash to your dog's collar and walk with her as she pulls the cart. Encourage her to forge ahead and gradually start positioning yourself closer to the cart.

4 Finally, sit in the cart and have your dog pull you. Reins are used for steering, and you can use your foot to brake if you need to.

WHAT TO EXPECT: Dogs vary widely in the time it takes them to learn this activity, but many dogs can be pulling within a month.

TIP: If at any time your dog spooks or does not perform confidently, go back to a previous step and continue to build his confidence.

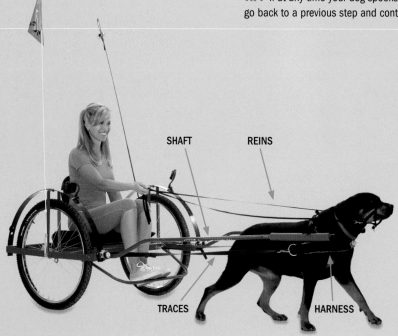

SHAFT   REINS

TRACES   HARNESS

1 Attach traces to your dog's harness and walk with her on a leash.

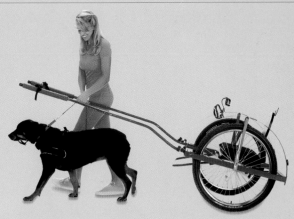

2 Hold the cart in your hand and walk with it trailing your dog.

Lift up on the shafts to allow your dog to escape, should she wish to.

3 Walk beside your leashed dog as she pulls the cart.

4 Sit in the buggy and have your dog take you for a ride.

OVERVIEW

In this extreme strength competition, dogs pull a weighted cart or sled a short distance.

American bulldog "Snow" pulls a sled carrying 900 pounds (408 kg) of weight to win the lightweight division of the Fur Rondy World Championship Dog Weight Pull in Anchorage, Alaska. The three-week winter festival began when fur trappers got together to trade and now includes dog competitions and other events to break up the long Alaska winter.

Weight Pulling

Weight pulling is a modern adaptation of freighting, in which dogs were used as draft animals to move cargo. In this competition sport, a dog in harness pulls a cart or sled loaded with weight.

The dog has 45 or 60 seconds (depending on the competition) in which to pull the cart or sled 16' (4.9 m). Wheeled carts are pulled over concrete or rails, and sleds are pulled across gravel, grass, carpet, or snow. Dogs are judged on the amount of weight they pull in comparison to their own body weight. In order to title, a dog has to pull eight times his weight on a natural surface or twelve times his weight on a man-made surface. The cart weighs 350 pounds (159 kg), which is therefore the minimum pull weight.

The handler may stand at the finish line and call to his dog or stand behind the cart and drive his dog. The dog's handler may not touch his dog, nor bait his dog with food or toys. If the dog is not able to pull the load (called a **no-pull**) the dog is eliminated from the competition. However, it is very important to the dog's self-esteem that he completes each pull. If a dog's owner senses a no-pull, he gives a signal to sled handlers who push the load from behind, thus letting the dog think he actually pulled the load.

GEAR

The **weight pull harness** is designed to disperse tension over a larger area of the dog. Its criss-cross styling and tension bar (which goes behind the dog and under the tail) greatly reduce the possibility of injury. The padded v-neck of the collar area pulls the harness down, away from the dog's throat allowing him to breath freely while pulling.

HOW TO GET STARTED

Drag weighting is used to condition the dog. The dog is taken on a medium distance walk (½ mile to 2 mile; 0.8 to 3.2 km) dragging a weight, such as a tire. This should be done on grass or dirt to provide adequate traction for the dog's paws.

MEET ROO YORI & WALLACE
WEIGHT PULL CHAMPION

"Wallace is a pit bull that I rescued from a shelter, where he was in danger of being euthanized. He had such high energy, that I decided weight pulling would be a good fit for him. I got him a harness and some weights and took him to the local park. I saw such a difference in him after our sessions, when his high work drive was satisfied. Wallace weighs 51 pounds (23 kg) and can pull a wheeled cart weighing 1,735 pounds (787 kg)!

"Wallace has become an ambassador for the pit bull community. We try to change the media perception and put forward a good image of pit bulls."

ROO'S TIP: "Weight pulling is a good exercise for high drive dogs. Condition your dog slowly and build a good foundation. If you push your dog too fast, you will burn him out."

IDEAL DOGS FOR THIS SPORT:

Many breeds participate in weight pulling competition, with dogs being separated into classes by weight. Sleddog and bull breeds excel within their respective weight classes, having been historically bred to pull. The most commonly seen breeds are American pit bull terriers, American bulldogs, Alaskan malamutes, and Rottweilers.

OVERVIEW

Teach your dog to swim alongside of you for a great partner exercise.

Open-water swimmers Kelly Reineking and "Chica" train in the warm waters of the Caribbean in the Cayman Islands. Chica is a mixed breed which Kelly refers to as a "Royal Cayman Brown Hound." (She says that it gives Chica an air of importance!)

Swimming

Swimming is a life skill that will benefit your dog through exercise and enjoyment playing in the water with you. Many public pools open their doors to dogs for a swim day at the end of summer, right before the pool is drained. Dogs can also swim at hunting dog retrieving ponds and indoor canine swim facilities, particularly ones that offer hydrotherapy (see page 76).

GEAR

A canine life jacket can make swimming easier by keep your dog from unwanted submersion and reducing fatigue.

HOW TO GET STARTED

Never force your dog into the water, either physically or by pressuring her socially by swimming away from her. Compulsion can escalate fear and create a serious water aversion.

Chose a warm, sunny day to teach your dog to swim and a location that is clean and safe with calm water and no threat of currents. It should have a firm, gradual walk-in water entrance. Check for dangers such as fish hooks, broken glass, debris, and water animals. If you have another water-loving dog bring her along so your non-swimming dog can watch her play.

Drop some floating treats into shallow water and praise your dog as she explores them. Wade into the water with some treats or your dog's favorite toy. Hold the treat or toy just above the water and a little ahead of your dog's nose. Let her walk into the treat or toy and have it—do not tease her by moving the toy away when she gets close.

The most challenging step will be the point where she crosses into swim depth, and it may take days or weeks of positive exposure to cross this point. Celebrate the moment your dog pushes off the bottom. If she begins to thrash, place your hand under her chest, lift up, and guide her back to shallow water. Avoid going deeper than waist-deep in the water so you can better control and help your dog.

Never leave your dog unattended, particularly in a pool, where it may be difficult for your dog to find the exit. Floppy ears can harbor infections when wet, and your swimmer will need regular ear cleanings.

MEET KELLY REINEKING & CHICA
OPEN-WATER SWIM RACERS, CAYMAN ISLANDS

"I've competed in sea swim races for fifteen years. My human training partners weren't always available and motivated for a swim, so I wanted a dog swim partner. I rescued Chica from the Humane Society when she was eight weeks old. At 11 weeks she fell off a boat into the water. I thought she would be traumatized, but she paddled to the surface, got out, and happily ran around, acting like swimming was the coolest thing!

"In this photo Chica earned a medal competing in an 800 m (0.5 mile) sea swim race. Chica came in 100th place out of 143 swimmers. Competitors judged their performance by whether or not they got beat by the dog!"

KELLY'S TIP: "Your dog will naturally swim right in front of you and even on top of you. A gentle nudge and a soft command such as 'no scratching' or 'just swim' and then LOTS OF PRAISE when they swim beside or out in front of you will bring the best results."

IDEAL DOGS FOR THIS ACTIVITY:

Breeds with webbed toes and buoyancy (lung capacity and fat to muscle ratio) are ideal swimmers. Newfoundlands and Labradors are more energy efficient at swimming than a whippet.

OVERVIEW

Paddle the open water
with your dog for a
stress-relieving, full-
body workout.

C.C. and her surfer dog "Diesel" are a
familiar sight at Waikiki Beach on Oahu,
paddling out from the beach in front of
the Moana Surf ider Hotel.

Stand-Up Paddleboard

A combination of surfing and kayaking, **stand-up paddleboarding** (**SUP**) offers an up close view of the water that even beginners can enjoy. Rhythmic paddling on thick, wide boards works every muscle in your body and offers a full-body workout.

Modern stand-up paddleboard riding got its start on the Hawaiian Islands. The board is similar to a surfboard, but it is wider, longer, thicker, and more buoyant. Riders use a long paddle to propel themselves and often have an ankle leash attached to the board in case they fall in the water.

When paddling with a dog, the dog is usually positioned in front of the paddler, close to her legs. When the paddler transfers the paddle from one side of the board to the other, she passes it over the front of the board. By having your dog close to your legs, you will be able to pass the paddle at a lower height over the board, allowing you to expend less energy.

GEAR

In addition to a board and paddle, a rubber deck pad will provide traction on your board. A dog life vest will keep your dog buoyant and easy to spot in the water.

HOW TO GET STARTED

Paddleboarding can be done by just about anyone, and many people can learn it after one 15-minute lesson. A small, protected channel provides perfect beginner conditions.

The first step is to teach your dog to swim (page 58). Next, accustom your dog to standing on the board and teach him how to climb back on should he fall off (page 68).

Use the instructions on the following pages to learn how to stand up on your board and get moving!

MEET JOY LEILEI SHIH & KALIA
HONOLULU, OAHU, HAWAII

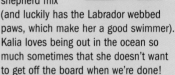

"Kalia is a border collie/Labrador/ shepherd mix (and luckily has the Labrador webbed paws, which make her a good swimmer). Kalia loves being out in the ocean so much sometimes that she doesn't want to get off the board when we're done!

"Stand-up paddleboarding has this sort of 'Huck Finn' adventure feel, which is great fun! It is so peaceful and amazing when you go far enough out that you no longer see other people, and it's just you and your dog. We've seen dolphins out there and even scalloped hammerhead sharks!"

LEILEI'S TIP: "Because stand-up paddleboarding usually means you go pretty far out from the coast, it's important that your dog is a strong swimmer. Paddleboarding requires good balance for both you and your dog—this takes practice—but eventually, you'll both get a feel for being on the board together!"

IDEAL DOGS FOR THIS ACTIVITY:

Any dog who enjoys being outdoors and is confident around water can enjoy paddleboarding.

Get started in the hot new sport of stand-up paddleboarding by learning how to get on top of your board and get moving.

MOUNTING YOUR BOARD:

First, get your dog on the board (see page 68).

1. While in shallow water, place your paddle perpendicularly across your board, behind your dog. Keep one hand on the paddle at all times, so that you don't accidentally lose it. Position the board to your right side. Place both hands midway on the board, with your right hand farther forward than your left.

2. In a smooth motion, slide your right knee onto the board so that the position of your two hands and your knee on the board forms a perfect triangle.

3. Pull your left knee onto the board, so that you are on all fours, facing forward.

4. Grab the paddle with both hands for balance, holding your hands shoulder width apart. Bring one foot to the spot where your knee was.

5. Bring your other foot up so that your feet are shoulder width apart and crouch to maintain balance.

6. Stand up and immediately begin paddling using continuous, long strokes on either side of the board, as it will be easier to balance when the board is in motion.

WHAT TO EXPECT: Your first trips should be very short and close to shore. Most people can be paddling after their first lesson!

TIP: Look forward rather than down to keep better balance.

1 With your board to your right, place your right hand forward of your left.

2 Slide your right knee onto the board, creating a triangle position along with your hands.

3 Pull your left knee onto the board.

4 Grab the paddle with both hands. Replace one knee with a foot.

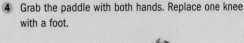

5 Bring your second foot onto the board and crouch to maintain balance.

6 Stand up and immediately begin paddling to maintain balance.

OVERVIEW

Enjoy nature with your dog as you kayak together on flat, calm waters.

Mixed breed "Brody" and his owner float down the Colorado River in Black Canyon, Nevada. Brody is appropriately equipped with his flotation vest. Brody's owner is more interested in getting a suntan.

Kayaking

Explore nature with your dog in a calm-water lake or inlet. You'll row your boat, and your pup can alternate between sitting in the kayak and paddling alongside it.

GEAR

Purchase your own dog life vest, as you want this to fit your dog very well. The life vest is used not only as flotation support for your dog but also as a hand-hold for getting your dog back into the kayak after he has had a swim.

Some kayak rental facilities specialize in dogs and rent appropriate equipment. There are several types of kayaks: single seat, double seat, and open board designs. All offer different options for taking a dog. A simple choice is a short, molded plastic sport kayak. The cockpit is wide enough that smaller dogs can sit between your legs with your legs inside the kayak. With a larger dog, hang your legs over the outside of the kayak and your dog can sit between your legs. Some dogs can learn to balance on the top of the kayak. Add traction to your kayak by gluing a non-slip, rubber surface in front of or behind the seat opening.

HOW TO GET STARTED

You'll want to be comfortable with your own kayaking skills and boat safety knowledge before involving your dog. Start by teaching your dog how to get in and out of the kayak from the shore. Hold the kayak still and pat it to encourage your dog inside. Once inside, instruct him to sit and stay. Don't allow your dog jump out of the boat until you give your release command, such as "off."

Slowly push the kayak and dog into the water a few feet (a meter), while keeping hold of it. Let your dog gradually get used to the sounds of oars bumping the side of the boat or paddles dripping water onto him. When your dog accepts riding in the boat quietly, pull the kayak back to shore and get inside with your dog and launch the boat. Go only a short distance at first and return to shore often. Later you can paddle or row around a little bit more each time, as your dog shows that he is comfortable.

Practice having your dog get into the kayak from deep water. Tie off the boat in waist deep water, sit inside, and either encourage him to jump inside or grasp his life vest and lift him in.

MEET LONNIE OLSON & SAIKOU & KOZI
KAYAKERS

"My brother is a serious kayaker (he even builds his own kayaks) and so he taught me the sport. I like to involve my dogs in everything I do, but I wasn't sure how to combine dogs and kayaks. So I went out and bought my own kayak and figured it out. My dogs and I have been hooked ever since!

"Saikou, my border collie mix, has been my kayaking partner for 12 years. Kozi, my boxer mix, hasn't gone out on the river yet, but we've been practicing in the pond."

LONNIE'S TIP: "Whenever my dog gets nervous and starts rocking the kayak in practice, I rock it more, and ask the dog to lie down. The instant she does, the kayak immediately goes still, and the dog learns that she's controlling the boat with her own movements. This teaches the dog what to do in a real rocky-boat situation—lie down and stay still."

IDEAL DOGS FOR THIS ACTIVITY:

Kayaking can be an enjoyable activity for all dogs who know how to swim. Dogs who are apt to chase birds and animals will have to be trained to "leave it" so they do not capsize the boat.

Dogs stand on surfboards (solo or with their owners) and ride the ocean waves. Surf's up, dawg!

Fox terrier "Murphy" (above) and cocker spaniel mix "TJ" (left) are stylin' in board shorts and shades as they "hang-8" at the annual Loews Coronado Bay Resort Surf Dog Competition in San Diego, California.

Surfing

To surf, a dog stands on the surfboard and his owner gives it a push so that it catches the wave.

Televised competitions draw hundreds of dog participants and thousands of spectators. Competitors are judged on length of ride, size of wave, catching a critical part of the wave, and maneuvers such as walking on the board, turns on the wave, hanging 8, barking, and kick outs. Additional points are awarded to unleashed dogs, dogs standing on the board (as opposed to sitting or lying), and a dog displaying a confident attitude. A **teams category** allows dog and owner to surf on the board together.

San Diego, California, is the dog surfing capital due to its dog-friendly beaches, including Del Mar and Dog Beach in Ocean Beach.

GEAR

A dog flotation vest or buoyancy aid is recommended. A dog surfboard should be soft on the top and the sides, with rubber fins and grip pads. A short 12" (30 cm) leash may be attached to the front of the board to pull the board into the surf. Many dogs dress the part with stylin' board shorts or bikinis, and shades.

HOW TO GET STARTED

Only teach surfing if you are comfortable swimming in the ocean, and your dog enjoys swimming—otherwise teach him something else. Start by teaching your dog to swim (page 58) and letting him get used to the waves and ocean environment.

See the instructions on page 68 for introducing your dog to standing on the surf board. During this lesson, your dog will, at some point, jump off the board into the water. When this happens, use a treat or your coaxing to try to get him to climb back on the board on his own.

Once your dog is comfortable standing on the board, it's time to dog surf. Chose a spot with small 1'–2' (0.3–0.6 m) waves, pull your board and dog out, and turn them around so they are facing toward the shore. When a wave comes, gently push the surfboard so that it catches the wave. Look for canine surf academies where you and your dog can get instruction.

MEET MICHAEL UY & ABBIE
PRESIDENT, SAN DIEGO DOG SURFING ASSOCIATION

"We surf every day after work. Abbie is a better surfer than I! She's figured out how to drop into a wave and even cut-out by herself. She's one of the few big wave riders; surfing waves that are double- or even triple-over-tail. Bow-wow-bunga!"

MICHAEL'S TIP: "Surfing requires tremendous trust between you and your dog. Don't undermine that trust by pushing your dog to do something she is not comfortable with."

IDEAL DOGS FOR THIS SPORT:

Water dog breeds enjoy swimming and being in the water. These include retrievers, spaniels, standard poodles, Portuguese water dogs, and Newfoundlands.

Dogs with shorter legs will have an easier time with their balance than leggy breeds. Herding breeds such as Australian kelpies, heelers, and border collies naturally "hunker down," which aids in their balance. Terriers have a "go get 'em" attitude that translates well into this sport.

STANDING UP ON A BOARD (PADDLEBOARD / SURFBOARD / WINDSURF BOARD)

1. Lay your board on the sand and guide your dog to stand on it.

2. Have four people lift the board a few inches (cm) off the ground and set it back down. Repeat several times.

3. Lift the board, walk it into shallow water, and set it down on the water.

LIFT YOUR DOG FROM THE WATER ONTO YOUR BOARD (PADDLEBOARD / SURFING / WINDSURFING / KAYAK)

1. Using the handle on your dog's lifevest, position her parallel to your board.

2. Build momentum by lifting your dog once ... twice ... and on the third time lift her onto the board.

3. Keep hold of her lifevest so that the momentum does not cause her to go off the opposite side of the board.

OVERVIEW

Toss a skimboard along the shore and your dog can jump on top for a short ride.

English bulldog "Tillman" skimboards on a beach in Ventura, California. Tillman also enjoys skateboarding and riding a snowboard.

Skimboard

A skimboard is a smaller, thinner version of a surfboard that is tossed along the shore after an incoming wave. It skims along the sand atop several inches of water, and the dog runs and jumps on top, riding the board for about 50 feet (15 m) until the wave disappears into the sand.

HOW TO GET STARTED

Some dogs will take to skimboarding, and others will have no interest in it (largely determined by breed). Let your dog watch as you skimboard and encourage him to chase after the board with you. Make it seem exciting. Next, toss the board and chase after it with your dog, but instead of jumping on it yourself, point to it and encourage your dog to "Get it! Get it!" If he steps on it at all, cheer excitedly and give him lots of praise.

MEET TILLMAN
SKIMBOARDING BULLDOG

Tillman loves to accompany his owner to the beach. His owner throws out the skimboard which Tillman chases until he can jump on with all four paws and ride the surf. He then picks up the board in his teeth and barks at his owner for another go. Tillman travels the country as the official spokesdog for a brand of natural dog food.

IDEAL DOGS FOR THIS ACTIVITY:

The same breeds that take to skateboarding will be ideal for skimboarding: bulldogs and small terriers such as the Jack Russell terrier.

OVERVIEW

If you windsurf, why not take your best buddy along for a wet and windy ride!

A Labrador retriever mixed breed dog rides on the bow of his owner's board in Oahu, Hawaii.

Windsurf

When windsurfing (or **sailboarding**) with your dog, your dog stands or lies down on the front of your board while you sail. You must have very solid windsurfing skills before you attempt to take your dog. The windsurf rig is heavy and can deliver a powerful blow to your dog if not handled securely.

GEAR

Use a large, high-flotation board with deck padding on the front. A dog lifevest is strongly recommended, providing not only flotation, but more visibility should your dog fall off your board.

MEET RAY MASTERS & SEVIN
MAUI, HAWAII

"I found Sevin abandoned, tied to a mailbox . . . on my birthday! He is a herding breed/terrier mix (I think.) He loves to be with me on the water—in fact he won't let me go out alone. We sail at high speed, fully on the plane, and pull off sharp carving gybes."

IDEAL DOGS FOR THIS ACTIVITY:

Small dogs such as the Jack Russell terrier fit well on the board and have the "go get 'em" attitude that allows them to enjoy "attacking" the oncoming waves.

If you're a skilled windsurfer and would like to take your dog along for a ride, teach him to be a safe and confident sailor.

Before introducing your dog to any water sport, teach him to be a confident swimmer (page 58). See the instructions on page 68 for introducing your dog to the board. Straddle the board in shallow water and let your dog get used to balancing on it.

Practice the self-rescue technique with your dog. Unfasten the outhaul, roll up the sail, and arrange the mast and boom over the back of your board. Paddle your board to shore with your dog on the board.

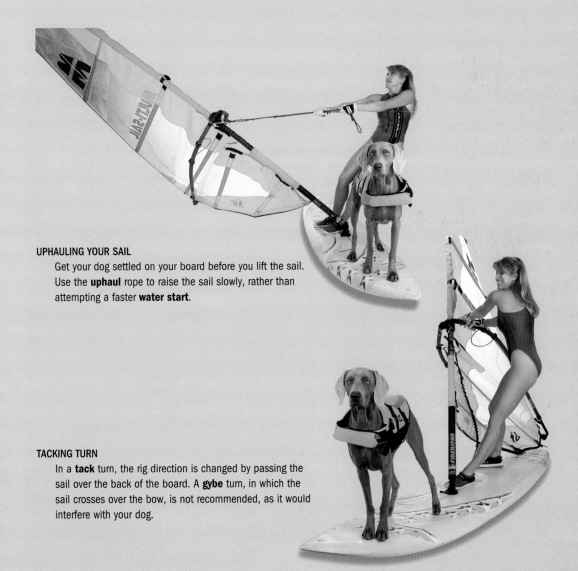

UPHAULING YOUR SAIL
Get your dog settled on your board before you lift the sail. Use the **uphaul** rope to raise the sail slowly, rather than attempting a faster **water start**.

TACKING TURN
In a **tack** turn, the rig direction is changed by passing the sail over the back of the board. A **gybe** turn, in which the sail crosses over the bow, is not recommended, as it would interfere with your dog.

Yellow Labrador retriever "Riley" leaps into a pool after his bumper toy during the dock diving All-Star Championships.

Dock Diving

Dock diving (also called **dock jumping** or **dog diving**) is a big air sport that even little dogs can enjoy. In this high-energy competition, a dog and handler work as a team to achieve the greatest distance jump for the dog. A variety of divisions allow dogs to compete against others of comparable skill level.

Dog and handler stand on a 40' (12 m) dock which is elevated 2'–3' (0.6–0.9 m) above a pool or lake. The handler tosses a toy (or **chase object**) off of the end of the dock to encourage his dog to jump into the pool after it. Each dog's jump is measured by the distance from the dock to the base of the dog's tail upon his entry into the water. In addition to the **long jump**, there are also categories for **highest jump** and **speediest retrieve**.

GEAR

The handler should have several of his dog's favorite toys to use as chase objects. Common toys are **flying discs**, **rubber bumpers** (photo below), **balls**, and **floating dog toys**.

HOW TO GET STARTED

Any dog can participate in this sport, and it doesn't require loads of training. Begin by teaching your dog to swim (page 58). The above-ground pool will have a ramp leading into and out of the pool. Work with your dog slowly until he is comfortable going from the ground, up the ramp, and into the pool. Help him find the ramp to exit the pool.

There are two common tactics that handlers employ to get the farthest jump. In **place and send**, the handler first throws the dog's toy into the pool. He then walks his dog back to the farthest end of the dock and releases him to run down the dock and into the pool after his toy.

The **chase** tactic is more difficult to execute but results in superior jumps when done correctly. The dog is told to "stay" at the back end of the dock. The handler stands at the front edge of the dock, calls his dog, and lobs the toy up in an arc over the water, just out of his dog's reach. This arc will encourage the dog to jump up, instead of flat.

MEET NADJA PALENZUELA & CLEMENTINE
PROFESSIONAL COMPETITIVE DOG SPORTS TEAM

"I never imagined that Clementine, my little 28 pound (13 kg) rescue cattle dog, could be competitive in dock diving. But when I took her to her first competition she knocked the socks off of her competition and almost won! Clementine isn't a natural water dog; her motivation comes from her desire to snatch toys out of the air."

NADJA'S TIP: "Don't ask your dog to jump into an unfamiliar body of water. Check the depth and let your dog walk into natural bodies of water before taking them onto a dock."

IDEAL DOGS FOR THIS SPORT:

Labrador retrievers are natural water dogs and traditionally dominate this sport. Other superior dock diving breeds include Chesapeake Bay retriever, Belgian Malinois, golden retriever, German shorthaired pointer, and border collie. There are also "lap dog" divisions for small dogs.

The current world record is held by greyhound/coonhound mix, "Country," who jumped 28' 10" (8.8 m).

OVERVIEW

Your dog can earn his water work title by demonstrating rescue skills such as delivering a life ring to a swimmer and towing a boat to shore.

Three-year-old Newfoundland "Whizz" leaps from a rescue boat as part of his training for the Royal Navy Reservists' Swansea rescue team. Whizz and his human handler rescue people from the waters of the Bristol Channel in South Wales, England.

Water Rescue

Throughout history there have been stories of dogs heroically saving lives in water disasters. Today strong, specially trained dogs and their handlers are used in sea rescue. The dog is equipped with a flotation device and sent to a distressed swimmer whom he then tows to shore.

Water rescue is also practiced as a sport, in which a dog can earn his **water work** titles. This sport is intended to encourage and test a dog's lifesaving instincts. Once a dog has achieved an advanced water work title, the handler can become CPR certified to then be considered a complete life-saving team.

The novice level **water dog** title consists of six tests: basic control on land; retrieving a bumper from the water; retrieving a life jacket; delivering a rope to a swimmer; swimming calmly with the handler; and towing a small boat 50' (15 m) to shore.

The advanced **water rescue dog** title consists of six tests: retrieving two articles in the proper order; leaping from a boat to fetch a paddle; discriminating between three swimmers and carrying a life ring to the one in distress; retrieving an item that is underwater (water is belly-deep to the dog); carrying a line from shore to a person in a boat and then towing that boat to shore; and leaping from a boat to save his handler who has "fallen" overboard.

The elite **water rescue dog excellent** title is earned through six tests: search for an abandoned boat and return it to land; rescue of multiple victims from the side of a boat; rescue of an unconscious victim; rescue of a victim under a capsized boat; delivering a line to shore from a stranded boat; and taking a line to multiple drowning victims.

HOW TO GET STARTED

Start by teaching your dog to swim (page 58). When a dog rescues a drowning person, he is taught to circle that person in the water so that the person can grab hold of his flotation harness. Teach this skill to your dog by having a person in the water give a treat to your dog each time he circles the "victim." Use a cue such as "go save."

MEET PAM SAUNDERS & HUDSON, PROMISE, MAKENA, CRUISER
WATER TEST MENTOR JUDGE

"I got my first Newfoundland, Aimee, 30 years ago and have been involved in water work ever since. Aimee, like many Newfies, loved the water but would get agitated if I swam out too far. She had a natural instinct to circle me while I was swimming and try to push me to shore. I would hang on to the hair on her hindquarters and she would pull me to shallow water."

PAM'S TIP: "Don't be afraid to take a step back in your training. A week before her certification test, my dog Makena suddenly refused to swim to the boat. I went back to using food treats and lots of happy praise to get her to swim just halfway to the boat, and it worked. That weekend she earned her title!"

IDEAL DOGS FOR THIS SPORT:

Many breeds can be trained to pass water work tests, however, the dog needs to be fairly large and strong. Newfoundlands were bred for water rescue work and have the size, strength, and webbed toes for this demanding work. Portuguese water dogs, Rottweilers, Leonbergers, and Labrador retrievers are also common in this sport.

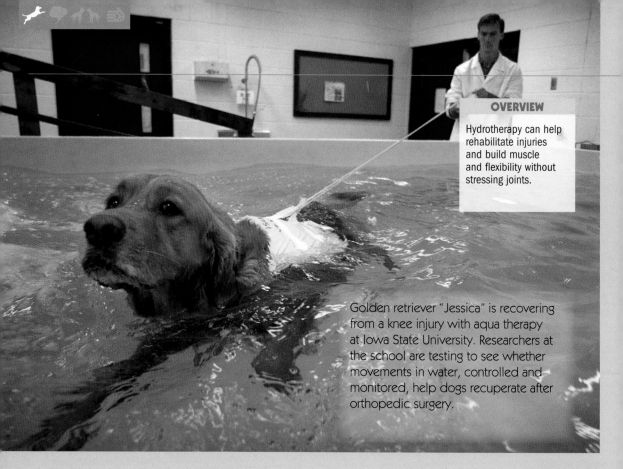

Golden retriever "Jessica" is recovering from a knee injury with aqua therapy at Iowa State University. Researchers at the school are testing to see whether movements in water, controlled and monitored, help dogs recuperate after orthopedic surgery.

Hydrotherapy

Hydrotherapy (or **aqua therapy**) is used in rehabilitation of injuries, treatment of chronic conditions, and in general fitness for dogs. The small pool is heated and may have jets to add resistance and encourage the dog swim more strongly.

While swimming, the dog moves through a full range of motion without weight bearing. This not only helps to rehabilitate the affected area but also keeps the rest of the muscles from becoming weak. For older dogs who have become reluctant to move, a swim in the pool can be a great way to get some exercise without stressing joints. Swimming in the warm water may also have a calming effect on your dog.

HOW TO GET STARTED

If your dog doesn't know how to swim, a technician will lend assistance. A veterinarian or technician can instruct you how to perform hydrotherapy exercises with your dog at your own pool.

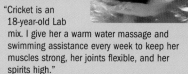

MEET CINDY HORSFALL & CRICKET
PRESIDENT, ASSOCIATION OF CANINE WATER THERAPY

"Cricket is an 18-year-old Lab mix. I give her a warm water massage and swimming assistance every week to keep her muscles strong, her joints flexible, and her spirits high."

CINDY'S TIP: "The dog needs to feel safe in the water. Hydrotherapy won't do any good for a dog whose body is full of stress."

IDEAL DOGS FOR THIS ACTIVITY:

Hydrotherapy can benefit older dogs, dogs who are injured or recovering from surgery, and the canine athlete (to cross train).

OVERVIEW

In this fun event, dogs race to swim across a pool chasing a lure pulled on a string.

Two Jack Russell terriers jump into the water chasing a lure at the Missouri Earthdogs annual muskrat races.

Muskrat Racing

Muskrats are medium-sized semi-aquatic rodents. In the past, dogs were used to swim after and catch the muskrats in an effort to control their population. Today's muskrat racing is a fun and humane sport, where dogs chase an artificial lure pulled by a string through a pool.

The dogs start on land and jump into the water after the lure. Dog **catchers** (often the owners) wait at the opposite end of the pool to help the dogs to the exit ramp. Designated doggy lifeguards are in the pool at all times. This is not a titling sport and is done merely for fun.

HOW TO GET STARTED

Dogs must be able to swim (see page 58). Improvised muskrat races are sometimes held at public swimming pools, at the end of summer right before the pools are drained.

MEET BETTINA WOOLBRIGHT & THOMAS

"Most of the dogs (like my Jack Russell terrier, Thomas) ran down the deck after the lure and didn't even realize there was water until they were in it! Some dogs put on the brakes right at the pool edge, and some still fell in from their momentum. Others just watched the lure float away and wouldn't jump in after it. Everybody had fun, and everybody got wet (owners too!)."

IDEAL DOGS FOR THIS ACTIVITY:

Jack Russell terrier events sometimes host muskrat races. It can also be found at dog fun day events. Dogs are sometimes classed by size.

A policeman and his yellow Labrador retriever sniffer dog search boxes for marijuana in an exercise in Cali, Valle del Cauca, Columbia.

Scent Detection Work

Canine scent work (also called **nose work** or **snifferdog**) is a recreational and titling sport that uses the dog's natural abilities to hunt for and locate a target odor. Inspired by the work of detection K9s, dog and handler teams have fun searching boxes, buildings, vehicles, and outdoor areas. It's a great way for a dog to have fun, build confidence, and burn mental and physical energy.

Scent work **trials** (titling competitions) use a variety of tests. In a **container search**, fifteen to twenty boxes are set up in rows. One of the boxes is the **target box** which contains the target odor (a cotton swab scented with either birch, anise, or clove oil). Each box is vented on the top with air holes. The handler and his leashed dog walk up and down the rows of boxes until the dog **signals** (usually by sitting or touching the box with his paw). The handler then calls "alert." Once the judge confirms the correct alert, the handler rewards his dog with a game of tug or with a food treat. Occasionally the dog will alert to a box directly next to the correct box, which is called a **fringe**.

Other tests include an **exterior area search** and an **interior building search**, in which the dog searches for multiple **hides** (objects with the target scent). The location of the hides is unknown to the handler. Another type of test is the **vehicle search** in which the handler must determine which of several vehicles contain the hide and its specific location. The difficulty of this type of search is to pinpoint the location as the odor, which is likely moving around and below the exterior of the vehicle. Handlers must help their dogs work to the source of the target odor before committing to an alert.

GEAR

Many handlers have a special toy that their dog really loves as a reward. They do not give the dog free access to this toy but allow her to have it only as a reward when she is working.

HOW TO GET STARTED

Start with three identical ventilated cardboard boxes. Hide a strong smelling yummy treat under one box. Let your dog explore the boxes, and as soon as she shows any interest in the correct box, praise her with a lot of enthusiasm, lift the box, and let her have the treat.

MEET BARBARA SCHWERDT & LANDIS
CERTIFIED NOSE WORK INSTRUCTOR

"I was volunteering at an animal shelter when I fell in love with a 14 week old German shepherd there. Landis turned out to be a challenging dog to own—he had intense drive and without an outlet for his energy was becoming destructive in our household.

"I started Landis in a 'Fun Nose Work' class when he was eight months old as a way to bond with him. Landis will do just about anything to get to his ball, so we hid his ball in a box and shuffled the boxes. To Landis, Nose Work is all about finding his ball at any cost!

"This sport saved my relationship with Landis by giving us a way to constructively utilize his need to work. By channeling his energy, Landis won all three titling competitions this year!"

BARBARA'S TIP: "Leave your obedience training at the door and let your dog hunt—really hunt!"

IDEAL DOGS FOR THIS ACTIVITY:

Dogs with long muzzles have superior scenting abilities to short-nosed dogs. Common sniffer dogs are bloodhounds, German shepherds, and Labrador retrievers.

Hounds have replaced pigs in sniffing out elusive truffle mushrooms from beneath the ground.

A truffle hound has found a tuber in Navarra, Spain.

Truffle Snuffling

Black truffles (a variety of mushroom) fetch a high market price and white truffles (**tartufo bianco**, or **white diamonds**), found only in Piemonte, Italy, and Croatia, can fetch extreme luxury prices. Since ancient times truffle hunters (**truffières**) used leashed, domestic truffle pigs to sniff out the elusive and expensive gourmet mushroom. Pigs have a keen sense of smell and a natural affinity for rooting in the earth for food. Unfortunately pigs also wanted to eat the truffles they found and at 300 pounds (136 kg) were difficult to pull away from the tuber. Today it is more common for dogs (known as **truffle hounds**) to be used for the job.

The fungi grow 2 to 24 inches (5 to 61 cm) beneath the ground on tree roots of willow, hazel, oak, poplar, and beech trees. They are harvested in the fall and early winter in the Northern Hemisphere.

In a typical Italian truffle hunt, the dog runs unleashed to and fro, nose to the ground, seeking out the scent of the truffle. Their sniffing is traditionally accompanied by the hunter's "Pei-la! Pei-la!" ("Go, get it! Go, get it!" in Piemontese). When the dog scents a truffle, he begins to scratch furiously at the earth. The hunter then removes the dog, digs up the truffle himself, and rewards the dog with a food treat.

Truffles grow in temperate forests all over the world, both wild and cultivated on farms. There are various truffle fairs, workshops, truffle dog training schools, and even truffle hunting competitions. In competition, dogs demonstrate their scenting skills and receive points for their aptitude, endeavour, and achievement.

HOW TO GET STARTED

Training a puppy may begin around 5 or 6 months of age and takes about three weeks. Dampen a tennis ball with truffle oil and toss it. When your puppy finds the ball, reward him with a tasty treat. After several days of training, toss the ball where your puppy can't see it, such as in grass, and let him search for it. Always reward him with a treat for finding it. As he gets better at using his nose, bury the ball under leaves or a little bit of dirt, so he will have to dig to get it. The scent will be easier for your dog to find if you leave it buried for a few hours, so the scent has time to permeate the ground. During initial training, allow your dog to eat a few truffles so he becomes more motivated to search.

MEET MARION DEAN & MUFTI
FOUNDER, TRUFFLE HUNTING CHAMPIONSHIPS, ENGLAND

"Far above the price of any truffle, I prize my relationship with my dog. Mufti is a lagotto, bred specifically to find truffles. Watching her work diligently and systematically through a quiet piece of woodland fills me with pride and admiration.

"On one occasion we knew we were very close to some extremely ripe truffles; the air was full of their heady aroma. It was obvious which tree was involved BUT, the tree was surrounded by a mass of thick brambles. There was no way I could have sent my dog in, as I didn't want her to get scratched up. There was only one answer—send in my husband instead. I was most impressed when he came out with two excellent truffles!"

IDEAL DOGS FOR THIS ACTIVITY:

Professional truffle hounds are not household pets; they are trained professionals and treated with great care and respect. The pups of a successful truffle hunter are extremely valuable. Commercial truffières often import the lagotto Romagnolo, an Italian dog breed bred specifically for truffle hunting. This ancient breed of water dog looks similar to a scruffy poodle and has webbed feet (see Mufti, above). Commonly, truffle hounds bear resemblance to dachshunds, poodles, fox terriers, and German shepherd dogs.

OVERVIEW

Enjoy the outdoors
as your dog sniffs out
the path traveled by a
human.

This experienced dog competes in a
Kennel Club Bloodhound Working Trial
in England. Called "hunting the clean
boot," the trials are a challenging and
exciting countryside activity in which
hounds follow a human scent trail over
a track up to 3 miles (4.8 km) long.

Tracking

As part of their hunting instinct, all dogs have the ability to **track**, or follow a scent trail. Dogs can be trained to follow the path traversed by a person or a prey animal.

Tracking trials (competitions) emulate the search for a missing person. In competition, a **tracklayer** walks through a field and drops an article of his clothing at the end of his track. In novice competition, the track is about 500 yards (0.5 km), with a few changes in direction. In advanced levels, the track is longer, has more turns, covers variable surfaces (asphalt, grass, dirt, or through a building), and is aged several hours.

The dog starts at one end of the track, following the scent trail and leading his handler. The trial is finished when the dog finds the article of clothing at the end. In British competition, the hound must also identify the tracklayer, who is standing in a line-up with two other participants. Identification usually takes the form of two muddy paws placed on the tracklayer's chest!

Tracking can also be done with a pack of dogs. In a British sport called **Hunting the clean boot**, a pack of bloodhounds follows the scent of a human runner (called the **quarry**). The term "clean boot" indicates that no artificial scent has been rubbed on the boots. The quarry sets out running an hour ahead of the pack and runs about 5 to 7 miles (8 to 11 km). The bloodhounds are given an article of the quarry's clothing to sniff and follow that scent. Following the dogs is the mounted field. When the hounds find their quarry they usually jump up and lick him.

Basset hounds, beagles, and dachshunds compete in breed-specific tracking **field trials** in which they track the scent of a hare. It is a bloodless sport, and the dogs are judged on their ability to track the scent. Coonhounds compete to track and tree raccoons.

GEAR

Dogs wear a tracking harness that allows them to pull, and worked on a 30' (9 m) lead.

HOW TO GET STARTED

Teach your dog to follow a track by using the instructions on the following pages.

MEET LISA WALLGREN & CHARLEIGH
RANCHER, TEXAS

"Charleigh was never a 'lay on the porch' type of bloodhound. We live on a 3,000 acre ranch, so I decided to put her instincts to work with tracking.

"When a deer is wounded, we need to find it quickly, and Charleigh can do it faster than we can. Once her head is down and her nose to the ground, her ears seem to turn off. I work her on a long lead or put a bell or remote tracking device on her harness.

"When Charleigh finds her quarry she is very proud of herself and lets the whole area know by baying up a storm!"

LISA'S TIP: "The tracking harness will be your dog's cue that she is working. Only put it on your dog for this purpose. Give the same verbal cues at the start of every session. I use: Ready? Go find!"

IDEAL DOGS FOR THIS SPORT:

Scent hounds hunt primarily by scent (as opposed to sight hounds). Most scent hounds have long noses, long ears (used to waft scent to their nose), and may have a hanging flew (bottom lip). Some scent hounds are bloodhound, basset hound, beagle, Catahoula leopard hound, coonhound, dachshund, foxhound, Norwegian elkhound, and Rhodesian ridgeback.

Teach your dog to use her nose to ground scent and follow a person's trail.

TRACK A PERSON'S SCENT TRAIL:

Your dog has an extraordinary nose and can track the path traveled by you or another person.

1. Lay your track in moist grass, where the scent will be easiest to detect. Scuff your feet at the beginning of your track to create a **scent pad**. Walk 50 yards (46 m) in a straight line, scuffing your feet along the way. As you walk, drop strong-smelling treats, such as hot dog pieces, every yard (meter). Use small cones or flags to remind yourself where you walked. At the end of your trail, place an object which has your scent, such as a sock. Stuff some treats inside the sock to capture your dog's interest.

2. Outfit your dog in a harnesses and 12' (3.7 m) lead. Bring her to the scent pad. Tell her to "track" and let her find the first treat left along your trail. Walk slowly, allowing your dog to pull forward. Do not reprimand her for veering off track but do not let her pull you off course.

3. When a working tracking dog finds a scented object, she is trained to signal the handler by lying down. When your dog gets to the end of your track and nuzzles the sock, tell her to lie down and reward her with a treat from inside the sock.

WHAT TO EXPECT: It is often hard to distinguish between a dog off-track and a dog picking up scent that has blown downwind. Take note of the wind direction, and if your dog is traveling downwind from your track, it may be that she is airscenting. Dogs enjoy scent work and can be tracking a trail of hot dogs within a few weeks. Once your dog is proficient, try a gradual 90-degree turn in your track.

TIP: Note that your track holds its scent for a day or more, so use a variety of training locations. Even when you are bundled up for cold weather your scent will come through your clothes. Your dog can also smell the scent of the smashed grass blades under your feet. If your dog is staying close to you and not leading, keep your lips zipped and let her instinct take over. The more you talk to your dog, the more she will look to you for direction.

1 Lay a 50-yard (46 m) straight track. Use cones to mark your path.

Drop a scented sock filled with treats at the end of the track.

2 Bring your dog to the scent pad to show her the scent she is to follow.

Let your dog pull as she searches for the treats left on the track.

3 When your dog finds the sock, have her lie down to indicate the find.

Reward her with a treat from the sock.

OVERVIEW

Trained volunteer dog/ handler teams assist in law enforcement requests to search for missing people, such as people lost in the wilderness or trapped by an avalanche.

Disaster Search Team Dan Solis and golden retriever "Gus" are trained to find people buried alive in the wreckage of disasters. Gus was rescued from a shelter and professionally trained for this work by a nonprofit organization. The organization ensures lifetime care for every dog in their program—once rescued, these dogs never need to be rescued again.

Search and Rescue

Trained volunteer search and rescue (**SAR**) dog/handler teams assist in law enforcement requests to search for missing people. **Wilderness dogs** use their scenting ability to track people lost in the wilderness. **Disaster dogs** are used to locate victims of catastrophic events (earthquakes, landslides, building collapses, and aviation accidents). **Avalanche dogs** search for people buried in the snow, and **cadaver dogs** are trained in human remains detection. Many disaster dogs in the United States are trained to meet the Federal Emergency Management Agency (FEMA) K9 standards. Volunteer groups conduct practice sessions to hone their skills and to help train new teams.

Dogs are trained to specialize in either airscenting or tracking/trailing. In **airscenting** the dog lifts his head and smells the breezes, searching for airborne human **skin rafts** (skin cells that drop off). Airscenting dogs typically work off-lead and cover large areas of terrain.

In **tracking** (page 82) the dog is trained to search for a human track by sniffing closely at the ground. They use clues such as crushed vegetation and disturbed earth to help them follow the track. **Trailing** is similar to tracking, except that the dog must also **scent discriminate**; follow the scent of a particular human (as indicated by giving the dog an sample of that person's scent).

GEAR

Dogs and handlers wear identifiable SAR vests. Tracking dogs wear a working harness and long line. Dogs may wear boots or other protective gear when working near collapsed buildings or areas heavy with debris.

HOW TO GET STARTED

The most important quality in a SAR dog is a strong **seek drive**. Tease your dog with a toy and throw it in a bush. A dog with a strong seek drive will keep searching until he finds the ball. SAR work is a game to dogs, and they are working in order to get a reward of a play session when they find their target. The play session can be a game of tug, a ball, or a food reward.

Initial training for puppies usually involves run-away games where the owner runs from the puppy and hides a short distance away. Initially the puppy locates the owner by sight, but later he learns to rely increasingly on scent to locate his owner.

MEET DAN SOLIS & SANDI
DISASTER SEARCH TEAM

"I became a firefighter because I wanted to help my community. Gus [photo left] was my very first search and rescue canine partner. Gus was rescued from the shelter and after one year of training he became nationally certified and partnered with me. He would spend the day with me at the firehouse and go home with me at night. Unfortunately our time together was short, and six months after our partnership began, Gus passed away from leukemia.

"Sandi, a border collie, is my current partner [photo above]. When Hurricane Katrina devastated the Gulf Coast, Sandi and I spent three weeks searching homes for live victims."

DAN'S TIP: "Be honest about whether this is something your dog likes to do. Be happy with what he is wiling to give."

IDEAL DOGS FOR THIS ACTIVITY:

Sporting breeds (such as Labrador retrievers and golden retrievers) and herding breeds (such as German shepherds and border collies) have a strong seek drive and work well with a human handler. Bloodhounds are the prototypical tracking/trailing dog. Newfoundlands and Saint Bernards are ideal avalanche rescue dogs.

Five-year-old bloodhound "Ellie Mae" works with her professional pet detective owner to search out missing pets. Together they have recovered many lost pets including a 60-year-old giant desert tortoise.

OVERVIEW

In this specialized form of search and rescue, a dog is used to find a missing pet.

Pet Detective

When a pet goes missing, specially trained search dogs can to follow the scent trail of the lost pet. The pet detective dog and handler use the same skills that are used in SAR (page 86) work, but instead of following human scent, they scent the lost pet's bedding and sniff out that animal's trail. Cat detection dogs are specifically trained to detect the airborne scent of cats.

Pet detectives can be paid professionals, or they can be volunteer lost pet search-and-rescue teams. They use police techniques such as search probability, forensics, and behavioral profiling to predict distances traveled by lost pets.

HOW TO GET STARTED

Play "hide-and-seek" games. Have a friend take a dog and hide. Encourage your dog to find his doggie friend.

MEET KAT ALBRECHT & CHASE
FOUNDER, MISSING PET PARTNERSHIP

"As a police officer, my police bloodhound and I worked to track people by scent. One day my police dog got lost in the woods, and I had an idea to use another police dog to track him down. It worked! Losing a pet can be devastating to an owner, and I enjoy helping people by recovering their lost pets."

IDEAL DOGS FOR THIS ACTIVITY:

The ideal trailing dog loves to play with other dogs and has a curiosity to use his nose. The best candidates for cat detection are dogs that love cats and become hyperexcited when they smell the scent of a cat.

A Jack Russell terrier enters a tunnel in pursuit of live quarry.

Earthdog

Certain terrier breeds, called earthdogs, were bred to **go to ground** to hunt vermin living in underground tunnels. **Earthdog trials** (also called **den trials**) are competitions that test this working ability and instinct. In competition, dogs negotiate through turns in a 30' (9.1 m) man-made underground tunnel, using their scenting ability to find the **quarry** (such as a rat) at the end of the tunnel. The quarry is protected in a cage and not hurt. The dog must reach his quarry within about 30 seconds and must **work** the quarry (bark and scratch).

HOW TO GET STARTED

Construct a short, wood tunnel with inside dimensions of 9" x 9" (23 x 23 cm). Toss a treat barely into the entrance. Your dog should tentatively stick his head in the tunnel and grab the food. Keep repeating this process, tossing treats a little farther inside. If your dog goes all the way through the tunnel, give him a whole handful treats.

MEET SHIRLEY LAMEAR & EDEN
EARTHDOG CLUB PRESIDENT

"I compete with Norfolk terriers (like Eden) and Jack Russell terriers. One hot day at a earthdog trial, my Jack Russell went in the tunnel but never appeared at the end. We opened the trap doors above the tunnels, but no dog. We couldn't figure it out. We finally found him waaay in the back, stretched out like a cat. Heck, that was the coolest place he had been all day!"

IDEAL DOGS FOR THIS SPORT:

Ideal dogs are dachshunds and small, short legged terrier breeds such as Jack Russell terrier, Norfolk terrier, border terrier, rat terrier, fox terrier, West Highland white terrier, Bedlington terrier, and miniature schnauzer.

A German shorthaired pointer finds and points a ring necked pheasant in Holland, Nebraska.

Pointing Game Bird

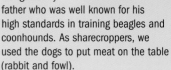

Sporting dogs (or **gun dogs**) were bred to locate and point birds for their hunting masters. Dogs **quarter** the field, running crisscross until they locate a **scent cone** emanating from a **bird covey**. The dog then **goes on point**; his body frozen, foreleg lifted, and nose pointed in the direction of the bird.

Dogs can earn titles by demonstrating their hunting instinct and training in noncompetitive **hunt tests** or competitive **field trials**. In hunt tests the dogs are judged against a standard, while in field trials the dogs compete against each other for championship points. Tests and trials simulate real hunting conditions on natural terrain, by hunting planted, pen-raised upland game bird (such as quail and chukkar). Dogs are run in **braces** (pairs) with a handler for each dog. At the junior-level, the dog must merely locate and point a bird. His handler flushes the bird and fires a blank shot from a **popper** (starter's pistol) to show that the dog is not **gun shy**. In the master-level test the dog must be **steady to wing and shot** (hold point while the bird is flushed and shot). Handlers carry unloaded shotguns to further simulate a real hunt, while official gunners shoot the flushed birds. If a dog encounters his brace mate on point, he must **honor** (hold still and allow his brace mate to work the bird). Judges and handlers sometimes ride horseback as the dogs **range** farther.

GEAR

Both handler and dog are required to wear some **blaze orange** clothing in a hunting environment. The handler uses a whistle (page 110) to direct his dog. During training, the dog runs dragging a 10'–12' (3–3.7 m) **check cord**.

HOW TO GET STARTED

Teach your dog four commands: heel, stay, come, and whoa. Hunting instructors use a remotely controlled **bird launcher** apparatus to teach a dog to hold point. The bird launcher holds a live bird. If your dog breaks point and busts in on the bird, the launcher springs the bird and it flies away. The dog learns that breaking his point causes him to lose the bird.

MEET JIMMY RICE
PROFESSIONAL FIELD TRIAL HANDLER, JUDGE

"As a boy, I worked alongside my father who was well known for his high standards in training beagles and coonhounds. As sharecroppers, we used the dogs to put meat on the table (rabbit and fowl).

"I later began competing in field trials and hunt tests and handle dogs in competition professionally. I feel fortunate to have been able to share my love of the dog and the hunting sport."

JIMMY'S TIP: "Eye contact with a dog is the most important thing. Your eyes click onto each other's, and it's like you hypnotize them. You and the dog have become one. When the dog is looking into your eyes, he's taking direction from you. When a dog won't look you in the eyes, it means he doesn't want to take your direction."

IDEAL DOGS FOR THIS SPORT:

Pointing breeds were bred for this sport, and include: German shorthaired/wirehaired pointer, Brittany, pointer, setter, spinone Italiano, vizsla, Weimaraner, and more.

OVERVIEW

Dogs are used to locate specific endangered an mals, plants, or animal scat for the purposes of conservation research.

Small Munsterlander pointer "Annie" locates young woodcock chicks, which her owner bands and releases as part of a volunteer nature conservation program.

A bird band is a small, uniquely numbered tag that is attached around the bird's leg. If a banded bird is found, the tag information should be reported along with details of where, when, and how it was found.

Wildlife Conservation Work

Dogs work for wildlife conservation in a variety of ways. Dogs locate living **endangered animals** (such as the Mojave Desert tortoise in Nevada) and they sniff out **threatened plants** (such as Kincaid's lupine in Oregon's Willamette Valley, host to an endangered butterfly). **Scat-sniffing dogs** locate scat of select species in a noninvasive manner, to be used for research purposes.

Thousands of volunteer owner/dog teams work every spring to locate woodcock (game bird) broods, record data, and band the chicks. This data is used by wildlife agencies to assess productivity, survival, and relative habitat quality for use in research and management projects. **Woodcock banding** is catch-and-release: The dog locates the bird in the field and points it; the handler captures the chicks with a net, measures their bills, bands them, and releases them unharmed. The woodcock hen will often feign a broken wing and flop around in an effort to distract the dog from her chicks, and the dog must be controlled to hold steady. Experienced banders searching good cover average two to three broods a day; a good day will produce five or six.

GEAR

Dogs may wear a small cowbell on their collar, informing the handler of where the dog is and how fast she is moving. Unfortunately the bell makes no sound when the dog is stopped and on point, making it sometimes difficult for the handler to locate the dog.

A dog may alternatively wear a beeper collar that beeps when the dog is standing still (presumably on point). On some collars, the beep sounds like a hawk screech, which serves to freeze the bird in place. Even when it is not hunting season, it is wise for both the dog and handler to sport some blaze orange clothing.

HOW TO GET STARTED

The banding of birds may require a federal banding permit, and some states require a state permit as well. In some states you may be required to spend a year's apprenticeship under an experienced bander to learn the ropes before becoming permitted. Contact your state's wildlife management department for information.

MEET DONNA DUSTIN & ANNIE
VOLUNTEER WOODCOCK BANDING TEAM

"I love woodcock banding because I get to spend spring in the woods with my dog. Annie was bred to hunt, and woodcock banding is like catch-and-release hunting. Annie and I work as team. The rush that I get after releasing the little fuzzball chicks is unbeatable."

DONNA'S TIP: "Teach your puppy self-restraint by having her 'wait' before going outside and 'wait' before getting food. If she doesn't, the door shuts or the food goes away. Puppies learn fast how to get what they want, and by teaching them that good things come to those who wait, you have a head start on training them to hold point later."

IDEAL DOGS FOR THIS ACTIVITY:

Pointing breeds such as the small Munsterlander pointer, Weimaraner, wirehaired pointing griffon, and German shorthaired pointer, as well as setters are used to locate birds for banding. Scat-sniffing, endangered animal, and plant sniffing dogs must be large and agile enough to search 4 to 5 miles (6 to 8 km) of demanding terrain per day, and have high drive. Herding breeds such as Belgian sheepdog or Tervuran will often work with intensity in order to get their toy reward.

This humane sport has taken the place of fox hunting. Hounds follow a scent trail artificially laid across the countryside.

Hounds set off from Great Budworth, England. Since the British ban on fox hunting, hunters now practice their sport through trailing a scented rag.

Drag Hunting

Drag hunting is an traditional cross-country equestrian sport, which has been in existence for more than 100 years. Drag hunting is not a blood sport, as no animal is hunted or killed, and has increased in popularity with new bans on fox hunting and blood sports.

In a drag hunt, instead of following the scent of a fox, a pack of scent hounds chase an artificial scent that has been laid (dragged) over the terrain. A **dragsman** lays scented **drag line** a half hour before the hunt by riding across the countryside, pulling along a scented rag. He may ride over small walls, fences, and hedges. When the hunt begins, the dogs run in a pack, followed by the **mounted field**. They follow the scent across the countryside until they find the dragsman at the end (and are rewarded with some biscuits). The dogs and riders have a rest as the dragsman leaves to lay another leg of the drag line.

While drag hunts follow a straight line and are designed for fast rides over marked jumps, **trail hunting** replicates the fox hunt more genuinely, with less predictable paths similar to the zigzag path of a hunted fox. There are breaks in the scent, and when a hound discovers an elusive trail again it will **give cry**, or bark and yowl.

Drag hunting has a reputation for being vigorous and requiring a high level of fitness and equestrian skill. This need not be the case, however, as the course can be tailored to the skill level of the participants, with routes around the more challenging obstacles.

GEAR

The drag scent is usually made up of animal urine or droppings to which paraffin is added as a fixative so that the scent doesn't evaporate, and aniseed is added to provide strength to the scent.

HOW TO GET STARTED

Because scent trailing is such an instinctual drive in hounds, they do not require much training in the sport. The hounds hunt as a pack, and a novice dog can be introduced into an experienced pack to learn the ropes. Teach your hunting dog how to track a short distance by dragging the scent through wet grass (which holds the scent extremely well). Leave a treat at the end of that trail to further encourage your dog to take to tracking. Read more about teaching your dog to track on page 82.

HUNTSMAN

The huntsman is responsible for directing the hounds during the hunt and has right of way at all times. His technical decisions must be quickly made, and staff and field must abide by them. The Huntsman carries a horn to communicate to the hounds, followers, and whippers. He makes sure that his hounds work together as a pack by steadying the **lead hounds** and encouraging the **tail hounds** to go faster. He directs his hounds by casting them in a certain direction.

WHIPPERS-IN

The Huntsman is supported by "whips" who bring up stray hounds and prevent the hounds from **riotting** (hunting wildlife.) They carry hunting whips (and in America they sometimes also carry .22 revolvers loaded with blanks).

IDEAL DOGS FOR THIS SPORT:

Originally foxhounds and beagles were used, but through selective breeding, trailhounds are now used because they are faster. Trailhounds look similar to foxhounds but are leaner in build. They originally were bred from foxhounds with other crosses to get a faster hound with a good nose.

Parson Russell terriers were bred to chase down vermin. This puppy satisfies his drive by chasing a tennis ball.

Fetch

Teaching your dog to fetch gives you a way to easily exercise him as the two of you play together. The more often your dog plays, the more obsessed he will become with this game.

GEAR

Choose a ball that is big enough ball that your dog cannot swallow it and soft so that it will not break your dog's teeth. Excessive mouthing of tennis balls can lead to tooth wear, so for chewers, a rubber ball is preferable.

HOW TO GET STARTED

1. Use a box cutter to make a 1" (2.5 cm) slit in the ball.

2. Show your dog as you drop a treat inside the ball.

3. Toss the ball playfully and encourage your dog to bring it back to you by patting your legs, acting excited, or running from him. Motivate him by chasing the ball yourself, batting it around, or bouncing it off walls. Make it a competition and race him for it. When your dog brings the ball back near you, gently take it and squeeze it to release the treat for him. As he is unable to get the treat out himself, he will soon learn to bring the ball back to you for his reward.

Some dogs will get the ball and run off with it. Never chase your dog when he is playing keep-away. Lure him back with a treat or run away from him to encourage him to chase you. Have a second ball to get his attention.

MEET DIANA JACOBS & NIKO SUAVE

"Niko is a 5 year old puggle (pug/beagle cross). Puggles do a half howl/half bark called a 'howrk'.

"Niko started fetching at 14 weeks. He really loves his ball. I work at a doggie daycare, and Niko comes to work with me. One day we decided to see how long he would play fetch before tiring of it. Boy did that backfire! I finally surrendered at 11:00 pm, after THIRTEEN HOURS of playing fetch!"

DIANA'S TIP: "Bring the ENTHUSIASM! If you're excited to play a game, your dog will be too!"

IDEAL DOGS FOR THIS ACTIVITY:

If you have a Labrador or a golden retriever, you've probably already discovered the hours of entertainment and activity this activity can provide. Sporting dogs and dog breeds with the word "retriever" in their breed names generally take to tennis balls and fetching games easily.

A dog and handler team compete for distance and accuracy in completing a catch.

"Beta" is a Catahoula leopard hound. A descendant of the red wolf, Catahoulas have unusual leopard-spot markings. Beta and her owner are professional disc dog performers. Disc play allows them to bond and also burn off some of Beta's crazy energy.

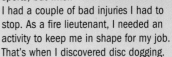

Flying Disc

Disc dog (also called **frisbee**) is a competition sport in which the handler and dog work together as a team to make as many successful throws/catches as possible during a timed round.

Geared toward beginners, the **distance/accuracy** event (also called **toss-and-fetch**) is played on a field marked with parallel lines spaced 10 yards (9 m) apart. The handler throws a disc from behind the first line (the **throw line**). Points are awarded for each successful catch the dog makes past the 20-yard (18 m) line. More points are awarded for catches made at longer distances. Extra points are earned if the dog is completely airborne for the catch. A round is 60 seconds and the team may only use one disc, so a speedy retrieval is helpful.

Long distance events are less common and have various formats, but generally the longest catch wins.

There are several disc dog competition divisions based on the skill and experience of the handler and include a novice division and a youth division. Men and women generally compete in the same divisions, although the long distance category is sometimes divided by gender. Small dogs compete in their own class.

GEAR

Use a flying disc designed for a dog: either a canvas or rubber disc or a plastic disc that is soft enough that it can be scratched by your fingernail. Hard plastic discs could injure your dog's mouth and teeth.

HOW TO GET STARTED

1. Introduce your dog to the disc by playing with it.
2. Get your dog's interest by spinning it upside-down in circles.
3. Then throw a "roller"—rolling the disc along its edge.
4. Toss the disc in the air for your dog to catch.

MEET MARK MUIR & WEELA
FOUR-TIME DISC DOG WORLD CHAMPION

"I had always competed in sports, but when I had a couple of bad injuries I had to stop. As a fire lieutenant, I needed an activity to keep me in shape for my job. That's when I discovered disc dogging.

"When I started out in disc I was ultra-competitive. It took me a while to figure out that it's not about me—it's about the interaction and bond with my dogs. My dogs have won ten world and national titles, but they'll never know it. They put their hearts into every competition, just for the fun of playing with me."

MARK'S TIP: "The more prey-drive play you engage in with your dog, the greater that drive will develop. Play ball or disc with your dog in small doses every day."

IDEAL DOGS FOR THIS SPORT:

Herding breeds that weigh in at 30–50 pounds (14–23 kgs) are natural disc doggers! Look for a dog with a lean build, sound hips, and strong retrieval and chasing instincts. Puppies under fourteen months should not be jumping for the disc, and all dogs should be checked by a veterinarian.

OVERVIEW

Dog and handler
execute high-skill
disc tricks in a
choreographed
routine set to music.

Red heeler mix "Five" vaults
off of his owner Tracy Custer
at a freestyle disc invitational
competition in Kokomo, Indiana.

Freestyle Disc

Freestyle disc is the pinnacle of competitive disc skill. Incredible flips, hyperfast multiple catches, and spectacular body vaults make this a popular event with spectators.

In a wonderful demonstration of teamwork, one dog and one handler perform a choreographed routine set to music. The routine is a presentation of tricks that involve different types of disc throws and catches. Some of the more spectacular tricks involve **vaults** (where the dog leaps off of the thrower to catch a disc) or **backflips** where the dog does a full revolution turn while catching a disc in mid-air.

During a ninety-second or two-minute competition routine, handler/dog teams are judged in categories including canine athleticism, degree of difficulty, showmanship, catch ratio, and multitude and variation of throws. Men and women compete in the same division, and there is also a pairs division in which two handlers and one dog comprise a team.

Routines vary widely, with some emphasizing tandem dance elements and others emphasizing highly athletic jumps. The team is allowed multiple (usually five to ten) identical discs on the field and the handler must fluidly collect the discs as a part of her performance. Human freestyle disc competitors are colloquially referred to as **disc doggers**.

GEAR

Read about the proper type of discs to use on page 99. Serious disc doggers sport a neoprene vest to protect them from scratches when their dog does a back or chest vault.

HOW TO GET STARTED

Before trying freestyle disc, your dog should be proficient at chasing, catching, and retrieving discs (see page 99). Always train on a soft surface that has good traction (lush grass is ideal). Avoid wearing sunglasses and seek eye contact with your dog often.

One of the key elements of freestyle disc is the **body vault**, in which your dog uses a part of your body (your thigh, back, or chest) as a launching pad to jump from in order to catch a high disc. The following pages will get you started on teaching a **back vault**.

MEET TRACY CUSTER
FREESTYLE DISC WORLD CHAMPION

"Most of my dogs are high-drive herding breeds, and I started disc play with them simply as a way to tire them out. Competing is not about the titles and the trophies but rather about the joy in playing together.

"Disc competitions are really fun, and the competitors are supportive. In this photo [left] I lost a bet to a fellow disc dog competitor, and so I had to wear a rival sports team's T-shirt while I competed. (And now this photo is printed in a book!)"

TRACY'S TIP: "Keep your play sessions short, fun, and always positive. Ending your disc session before your dog loses interest will help to build drive and desire to play."

IDEAL DOGS FOR THIS SPORT:

A freestyle disc dog should have strong chasing and retrieval instincts, sound hips, and a lean build.

Herding breeds such as border collies, McNabs, Australian shepherds, cattle dogs, and Belgian Malinois are the most common breeds in this sport. Sporting breeds and terriers tend to have a strong chase drive which is advantageous in this sport. Small breed dogs can compete in a "micro freestyle" division.

Teach your dog to get big air by vaulting off your back to catch a disc.

BACK VAULT:

Your dog should be at least fourteen months old, free of injuries and physical problems, and in proper weight. Always work on a surface with good traction and a soft landing, such as lush grass.

1. Wedge sand bags on either side of a barrel to hold it steady. Use a treat to lure your dog to jump on top. Let your dog have the treat while he is on the barrel.

2. After a few repetitions, lure your dog as before but then toss the treat forward about 8 feet (2.4 m) to encourage a horizontal jump.

3. Put on protective gear such as a neoprene (wetsuit material) vest, so that your dog doesn't scratch you. Lay your body across the barrel and cue your dog as before. Toss the treat in front of him as before.

4. Continuing in the same session, remove the barrel and have your dog vault off of your body.

5. After about 50 repetitions over the course of a week, it is time to introduce the disc. Teach your dog to catch a flying disc (page 99). Then have your dog do a **take** (take a disc from your hand) in combination with the back vault. Finally, toss the disc and have your dog launch off of your back to catch it!

WHAT TO EXPECT: Dogs can learn the first four steps within a few weeks. You will need to practice your throws on your own.

TIP: If your dog scratches or hurts you, don't let on, as he will be reluctant to do a behavior that he thinks is hurting you.

1. Use a treat to lure your dog on top of the barrel. Let your him have the treat while his is on top.

2. Toss the treat forward as soon as your dog jumps on the barrel.

3. Lay your body across the barrel and cue your dog as before.

Toss the treat front of him as he jumps.

4. Remove the barrel and have your dog vault off just your body.

5. Introduce the disc and have your dog take it from your hand.

English bulldog "Tyson" began chasing after kids on skateboards when he was just a few months old. On his first birthday, Tyson was given a skateboard and immediately began standing on it and pushing himself along.

Skateboard

It's a skater dog! Teach your bud to shred and he'll be sure to turn heads at the skate park. There are several ways your dog can skateboard. He can stand on the board while you pull it with a leash; he can jump on the board and coast and jump off; or he can actually move the skateboard with his foot. Skilled dogs can even bank turns.

GEAR

Most dogs will be able to ride a regular large skateboard, which you can buy from a toy store. For larger dogs you can use a longboard, which is about 35" (90 cm) in length and is flat, without the normal flipped tail.

HOW TO GET STARTED

Some dogs (largely determined by breed) become quickly fascinated with the skateboard and practically teach themselves to ride it. Other dogs need more instruction from their owners.

1. Start by getting your dog interested in the skateboard. Roll it, skate on it yourself, and encourage him to chase it and play with it. Keep up your enthusiasm and praise your dog for any interaction he has with the skateboard. After several weeks you should be able to tell if your dog is a natural skateboarder (showing a lot of interest in chasing the board) or if he needs to be taught this behavior.

2. To teach your dog to ride a skateboard, start by holding the board still with your foot and using a food treat to lure your dog to put his front paws on the board. Give him a treat when he does.

3. Once he is comfortable with this, move the board a little, either with your foot or with a leash attached to the front axle.

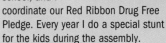

MEET DALE ANDREOLI & BONY HAWK
SKATEBOARD PERFORMERS

"I'm a teacher at an elementary school, and I coordinate our Red Ribbon Drug Free Pledge. Every year I do a special stunt for the kids during the assembly.

"One year I thought I'd try a stunt of a skateboarding dog. I bought an eight-week-old bulldog puppy and named him 'Bony Hawk' (after the pro skateboarder, Tony Hawk.) The first day I brought him home, he got on the skateboard and took off!

"Bony Hawk was a hit at our assembly, and has gone on to perform at fairs and events. He even has his own ID card at the skatepark."

DALE'S TIP: "I've never used training treats with Bony Hawk. Whenever I want to get him excited about skateboarding, I pound the skateboard on the ground and he goes crazy!"

IDEAL DOGS FOR THIS ACTIVITY:

Many bulldogs take to skateboarding naturally and have a prey-drive desire to chase it and ride it. Their short legs, wide stance, and low center of gravity make it easier for them to balance. Other bull breeds are also good candidates for this activity, as well as small terriers, including the Parson Russell terrier.

Set up a tetherball pole and let your dog jump and bop the ball for fun and exercise.

Tetherball is Australian shepherd "Jackson's" favorite game. He will play it by himself or with his dog friends.

Tetherball

Tetherball is a great way to let your active dog burn off excess energy and to encourage your sedentary dog to get moving. Many dogs really enjoy bopping the ball around the pole and will play by themselves or take turns with another dog.

GEAR

A regulation tetherball and pole seem to be the favorite for dogs, but you can also hang a ball on a bungee cord from a tree branch. Hang the ball at nose height for your dog.

HOW TO GET STARTED

Play with the ball yourself to encourage your dog to play. Toss the ball away from your dog and not at him. When he noses the ball, praise him excitedly.

MEET CHUCK GOODENOUGH & KAIBAB

"I bought Kaibab, my Aussie/heeler mix, at a rodeo. His littermates were free, but because he had one blue eye he was $25. Kaibab plays tetherball for ten minutes, lays down and rests, and then goes at it again. Sometimes he is standing there, sees the tetherball out of the corner of his eye, and jumps on it! Sometimes he jumps so hard he flips himself over! He makes funny growling noises when he plays."

IDEAL DOGS FOR THIS ACTIVITY:

Ideal dogs are ball-crazy with lots of prey-drive. Herding breeds, bull breeds, boxers, Rottweilers, and even little Pomeranians enjoy tetherball.

OVERVIEW

Dogs with herding instincts love to play with a soccer ball and even learn to roll it into a net. Score!

Border collie, "BEK" (named after soccer superstar David Beckham) enjoys chasing the soccer ball and bringing it back to his owner who is waiting at the goal net. BEK started playing soccer at nine weeks of age.

Soccer

Some dogs are fascinated by soccer balls and enjoy chasing it and moving it down the field. Commonly the owner will kick the ball and the dog will chase the ball and navigate it back to the owner.

GEAR

Dogs will play with regular soccer balls; however, if you find your dog is puncturing the ball, switch to a hard, plastic ball.

HOW TO GET STARTED

If your dog is not interested in the soccer ball on his own, use a treat dispensing ball. When rolled, these balls randomly let treats fall out. Fill the treat ball with dog kibble and allow her a few days to play with it on her own—it will likely become a favorite toy.

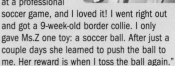

MEET MARK LUKAS & MS.Z & BEK
PROFESSIONAL SOCCER DOG ENTERTAINERS

"Ten years ago I saw a soccer dog at a professional soccer game, and I loved it! I went right out and got a 9-week-old border collie. I only gave Ms.Z one toy: a soccer ball. After just a couple days she learned to push the ball to me. Her reward is when I toss the ball again."

MARK'S TIP: "Practice soccer in a hallway because the ball only goes forward and backward."

IDEAL DOGS FOR THIS ACTIVITY:

Herding breeds (such as border collies and Australian shepherds) often instinctively like to "herd" a soccer ball.

At this IronDogs camp, campers participate in agility, dog dancing, tricks, disc, and flyball lessons, as well as nature hikes and training seminars.

Dog Camp

Dog camps are a great way to explore new dog activities, bond with your best buddy, and make new dog-loving friends. Camps last several days and feature a variety of sport training workshops, seminars, and clinics taught by expert trainers. Camps are often in the woods, with campers sleeping in tents or cabins.

Exposure camps are a novice introduction to a wide variety of dog sports, often including such favorites as agility, flyball, disc dog, dock diving, canine freestyle, and dog tricks. Multiple classes and seminars are scheduled throughout the day, and each student chooses which classes to attend in each time slot.

Skills camps focus on a specific sport, such as agility or sled dog, often catering to people at competition level looking to improve their skills.

KYRA SUNDANCE
DOG CAMP INSTRUCTOR

"Campers and their dogs learn a ton of stuff at camp, but more than that, it is a wonderful bonding experience. There is nothing like sharing a sleeping bag with your dog to bring you closer together!"

IDEAL DOGS FOR THIS ACTIVITY:

Dogs are in close contact with each other, so dog-aggressive dogs are usually discouraged from attending.

OVERVIEW

Your dog can earn merit badges for a variety of skills. Working toward a goal will keep you motivated to train.

Blue tick beagle "Bear" ("Baron von Beaglestein") has earned many merit badges including lure coursing, agility, and paw painting.

Dog Scouts

Not all people enjoy competition, nor do all dogs. But having goals to work toward drives our training and motivates us to try new things. Dog scout merit badges can provide these goals.

Dogs earn badges for learning a new skill and performing it according to defined criteria. There are badges for things such as backpacking, boating, steeplechase, scent discrimination, and paw painting. Dogs do not compete against each other but rather strive so achieve a goal.

HOW TO GET STARTED

Dog scout **troops** organize dog camps at which they introduce you to new activities and help you in their instruction. Troop leaders can evaluate your dog's skills and award merit badges.

MEET CHRIS PULS & BEAR & COYOTE
PRESIDENT OF DOG SCOUTS

"Bear has 24 scout badges, and Coyote has 50! Earning badges gives me goals I can achieve without having to enter a competition and perform for an audience. The first specialty badge my dog earned was for paw painting. I smile every time I see my Rottweiler's painting, and it is even more special to me now that he's gone. It may not look like art to most people, but to me it is a priceless masterpiece."

A competitor at a working dog field trial g ves whistle commands to her Labrador retriever.

Whistle Train

Whistles are used in dog training in place of verbal commands when the dog is working at a distance. Whistle commands are most commonly seen in the sports of hunting/retrieving and herding, where the dog ranges a significant distance from his handler.

The general convention in whistle training is to use one single note to discourage a dog's activity (similar to the word "whoaaaaaa...") and repeated staccato notes to encourage activity (similar to "tut tut!"). See charts below for conventional whistle commands.

GEAR

Hunting dog whistles are the standard "traffic cop" style, while herding whistles are semicircle or triangle.

HOW TO GET STARTED

Teach your dog to "come" to a whistle command. Assuming your dog already understands the verbal cue "come," it is easy to teach him to respond to the whistle. Blow your whistle in a distinct pattern that you wish to represent this command (see charts below for ideas) and then say the word "come" (always blow the whistle *before* you say the verbal cue). Reward your dog for coming. Soon you will be able to drop the verbal cue and just use the whistle command.

MEET HUBERT BAILEY & JOSÉ HERDING DOG BREEDER, TRAINER, AND CHAMPION

"I whistle with just my lips, and my whistle commands can be heard a mile away. A good whistler can control the tone and pitch of the whistle and use it to communicate more effectively than he could with his voice. If you're slowing down your dog, for example, you can give him four or five whistles that change slightly in velocity. The harder and shriller the whistle, the faster the dog will slow up.

"Sometimes I will work 4 or 5 of my dogs at the same time and have unique whistles for each dog. For one dog, I use a 'shooting star' whistle to mean 'go right' and a 'one side of a box' whistle to mean 'go left.' For another dog I use different whistles. Each dog knows his own whistles and ignores the others."

HUBERT'S TIP: "When you choose your whistles, choose ones that sound very different, especially in their initial sound."

HUNTING WHISTLE COMMANDS:

Come	Series of double or triple tweets and arms outstretched to your sides
Stop hunting and look at the trainer	One long blast
Sitting the dog at a distance	One long blast with your hand raised and open
To redirect the dog	"Pip-pip" (sharp and crisp) and the new direction indicated with your hand

HERDING WHISTLE COMMANDS:

Come	"Tweet-tweet-tweet" (rising at the end of each tweet)
Stop/Lie down	One long blast
Walk up/Move toward the livestock	"Pip-pip" (sharp and crisp)

This positive training method is extremely effective in teaching new behaviors to a dog.

Yellow shepherd "Jackson" is a quick learner. Her owner uses clicker training to teach her new behaviors.

Clicker Train

Clicker training (or **marker training**) is widely used in training animal actors, service dogs, and in training obedience, agility, dog dancing, dog tricks, and a wide variety of other activities.

The crux of clicker training is teaching a behavior by *clicking* a noisemaker at the exact moment the dog performs the desired behavior. This pinpoints for the dog the exact thing she did that was correct. It helps her to understand the desired behavior so that she can repeat it. A common misconception is that the dog is rewarded by a *click* instead of with a treat. This is not the case. The dog is taught that every *click* results in a treat. The dog is still working for treats. The *click* merely pinpoints a behavior very precisely.

Instead of a clicker, you can use a unique word (such as "yes!" or "good!") as your reward marker sound. A clicker tends to be especially effective, however, because it is very sharp, consistent, and distinct from our voices.

GEAR

A clicker is a handheld gadget with a metal tongue that makes a *click* sound when pressed. Clickers are available at pet stores. Use a flexible strap or rubber band to attach it to your wrist for easy access.

HOW TO GET STARTED

The first step in clicker training is to teach your dog to respond to its sound. Do so by building the association between the *click* sound and the food reward. This is called **charging up the clicker**.

1. Put twenty small treats in your pocket. Walk around casually near your dog but do not give her any instruction. Occasionally, and at random intervals, click your clicker.

2. After clicking, immediately (within two seconds) give your dog a treat. This will build the association between the *click* sound and the food treat.

WHAT TO EXPECT: Within a few minutes (and maybe twenty clicks) your dog should be responding to the clicker and spinning his head toward you when he hears it. You can now use this tool to *click* and treat any behavior that you wish your dog to repeat.

MEET JOEL NORTON & DUKE
HEAD STUDIO TRAINER, ANIMAL ACTOR AGENCY

"I first learned clicker training while working with exotic animals in college. Now, as a professional studio trainer, I use a clicker to train dog actors. When I'm teaching a dog to back up, I start by clicking the dog for moving even one foot backward. Once he gets the hang of that, I'll up the ante and not click until he takes two steps backward. Eventually I'll have the dog backing up all the way across the room before I click!"

JOEL'S TIP: "Timing is everything. When a dog is learning a new behavior, he may be moving around and trying all sorts of things. Try to click at the precise instant he did the right thing."

TIP:
Once your dog has learned to respond to a clicker, you can use this tool in training. There are three rules to using a clicker:

1. Click to mark any behavior you wish encourage.

2. Click the instant the correct behavior happens.

3. Each click is followed by a treat (no multiple clicks).

Click

OVERVIEW

Dogs respond readily to hand signal cues. Teach your dog the signals for common behaviors.

A competitor at a working dog field trial gives hand signal commands to her Labrador retriever.

Hand Signals

Hand signals are used to give commands (or cues) to a dog. They are used in a variety of training activities such as in competition obedience, on set with animal actors, in retrieving competition when the dog takes direction at a distance, and with deaf dogs. Most dogs respond to hand signals more readily than to verbal cues and when presented with conflicting cues will follow the one indicated by the hand signal.

Hand signals are not arbitrary and are usually born from the initial luring pattern used when training the dog. A downward hand motion is used to signal **down** and parallels your initial luring of your dog near the floor. The hand signal for **sit** is similar to the upward baiting of a dog that we do in his initial training of this behavior.

MEET KARA GILMORE & SQUIRT

"Squirt was deaf when I adopted her as a puppy. Since she couldn't hear me, it was crucial that I teach her to focus her eyes on me. I spent our first month working on nothing but eye contact.

"I use hand signals to communicate with Squirt. Instead of using a clicker, I do a thumbs-up for a reward marker. Squirt is a world-class disc competitor and when she performs, the crowds wave their hands above their heads to show they are cheering for her!"

FOCUS	SIT	DOWN	STAY	COME

STAND	HEEL	SHAKE HANDS	BOW	SPIN CIRCLES

BEG	ROLL OVER	BARK	DIG	COVER EYES

TEACH HAND SIGNALS:

Above are some common hand signals. If your dog already knows the verbal cue for a behavior and you wish to teach him the hand signal, teach him this way:

1 Always give the unfamiliar cue before the familiar cue. First give the hand signal [unfamiliar to your dog] . . .

2 . . . and a second later give the verbal cue [familiar to your dog].

3 Reward your dog when he correctly does the behavior.

4 Over time, your verbal cue will no longer be necessary, as you will find that your dog does the behavior already at your hand signal.

WHAT TO EXPECT: Because your dog wants the reward as quickly as possible, he will learn that a particular hand signal always precedes a particular verbal cue, and he will learn do the behavior already at your hand signal (thus getting his treat quicker).

A golden retriever in Devon, England recovers a
downed pheasant for his hunting master. This dog
was rescued from a shelter and it is his first year
"picking up" (collecting the pheasants) after they
have been shot by the "Guns" (hunters).

Field Retrieving

Dogs are used to retrieve downed birds when hunting (typically in waterfowl hunting but also in upland game bird hunting).

Retriever hunting tests provide a way to demonstrate your dog's retrieving instinct and training and to earn titles. In the junior-level hunt test, the dog needs to retrieve a downed bird on land and in water. At the sound of a gun shot, a dead bird is thrown in the air by a **bird boy**. The owner is confined to a marked circle of 12' (3.7 m) in diameter, and the dog must find the bird and deliver it to his owner's hand.

At the master level hunt test, the dog must hold steady and watch his owner's gun as multiple birds are shot. The dog must **mark off the gun** and remember where each downed bird (**mark**) has landed. Once shooting has ceased, the owner commands his dog to retrieve each downed bird. If the dog did not see the bird fall, he must do a **blind retrieve** and find the bird by taking direction from his handler via hand signals (page 118) and whistle signals (page 110). The handler whistles to command his dog to sit and look at him. He then extends an arm to his right or left to indicate the direction his dog is to travel.

Field trials are very similar to hunt tests but are competition events at which dogs compete against each other for championship points. The retrieves are farther, sometimes in excess of 250 yards (230 m), and more difficult. Dogs score points in natural retrieving desire, memory and marking ability, and obedience to their handlers' commands.

GEAR

Humans and dogs are required to wear some **blaze orange** clothing in a hunting environment. The handler uses a whistle to direct his dog. The dog may wear a chest protector for protection against the brush. **Retrieving dummies** (or **bumpers**) scented with bottled bird scent are used in training. (See page 118 for photos of gear.)

HOW TO GET STARTED

Encourage your dog whenever he is carrying an object. Don't take the object immediately from him but allow him to carry it near you. You don't want your dog to think you will take his possessions from him, or he will be reluctant to bring you a bird.

Use the instructions on the following pages to teach your dog directional retrieving.

MEET MARTIN DEELEY & TWO DOT
UK GUNDOG TRAINER OF THE YEAR

"Many years ago when I first started hunting, my spaniel, Ben, was supposed to be searching for a lost downed pheasant, but he kept disappearing into a rabbit hole instead. I got frustrated at him for becoming distracted by the rabbit smell. After sending him for the third time to find this bird, a more experienced dog handler walked up and asked me what was happening. I explained the situation, upon which he smiled, and proceeded to put his hand down the rabbit hole. He pulled out the pheasant. 'Trust your dog, son'—the words have echoed in my head for almost 35 years."

MARTIN'S TIP: "When your dog is carrying a object, briefly take it, rub it with your hands, and give it back to him so your smell becomes associated with something friendly and fun. If he picks up something of yours, get down low, encourage him to you, and let him know he is a 'good boy' for bringing it to you."

IDEAL DOGS FOR THIS SPORT:

Retrieving breeds often have the word "retriever" in their name, such as Labrador retriever, golden retriever, Chesapeake retriever, Nova Scotia duck tolling retriever, and flat-coated retriever. Standard poodles are also considered a retrieving breed. Many pointing breed clubs host retrieving competitions and titling programs as well.

Direct your dog by **casting** her with your arm signal.

① Hold your left hand in a "stay" signal and toss the bumper with your right.

② Blow your whistle. When your dog looks at you, cast her right.

③ Place bumpers on either side of your dog. Do not accept an incorrect retrieve.

④ Raise your hand straight up to signal your dog to go away from you.

DIRECTIONAL CASTING:

Before training this skill, teach your dog to fetch (page 96), stay, come, and to sit upon a whistle command (page 110).

① Work on each cast separately. Place your dog on a sit-stay facing you and attached to a long-line. Rubber hunting **bumpers** (also called **training dummies**) are used in retrieval training. With your right hand, toss a bumper to your right. Keep your left hand held in the "stay" signal. If your dog runs for the bumper, use the long-line to stop her, and place her back in position.

② Blow your "sit" whistle. When your dog looks at you, cast with your right hand and command "fetch, over." Praise your dog for retrieving the bumper. After five successful right-hand retrieves, teach left-hand retrieves, casting with your left hand to your left side.

③ Next, place a bumper (or pile of bumpers) on either side of your dog, about 10' (3 m) away. We are now eliminating the excitement of the throw and asking the dog to retrieve on command. Cast her to one or the other direction. If she goes in the wrong direction, immediately try to stop her by whistling her to "sit." If she brings the bumper from the wrong pile, do not accept it and place her back in the starting spot.

④ Teach a **back cast**. Place a bumper (or pile of bumpers) 10' (3 m) behind your dog. Raise your hand straight up and command "fetch, back."

WHAT TO EXPECT: Avid retrievers can start to pick this skill up in a week. Simulate real-world hunting by throwing a bumper or bird-scented dummy off in the distance and using directional signals to guide your dog to it.

TIP: If your dog does not enjoy retrieving, you can still practice this skill by setting up platforms to your dog's right and left and directing her to jump on one or the other. Give her a treat when she does.

SIT-WHISTLE POSITION

At a distance, your dog needs to see clear directional signals from you. A field cast should originate from the center of your body. Hold your hands over your torso until you give the cast, and then shoot your hand straight out or straight up in one quick motion (it is easier for a dog to see a quick movement, rather than a stationary position). Your signaling arm should be far from your body to create a larger visual picture.

OVER CAST

You can augment the **over** cast with sideways body motion.

BACK CAST

In a **back cast**, the dog is directed away from the handler.

COME-IN

Bring your dog toward you by using a whistle to call your dog to **come in**. Once she starts moving toward you, you can toot the sit-whistle and give her a new cast or wait for her to come all the way in to you.

MARK AND SEND

With your dog by your left side, use your left hand to **mark** the direction of the bird and **send** your dog.

"Chica" is a blind and deaf Australian shepherd. Many double-merle Aussies who are born white are blind and deaf (called lethal whites) and are destroyed. With training, these dogs live and function just like any other dog.

Teaching a Deaf or Blind Dog

Socialization with dogs and people is extremely important for a blind or deaf dog and should be encouraged. Blind dogs are taught to respond to verbal cues, while deaf dogs are taught to respond to hand signals (page 114). Touch signals are used for a dog that is both blind and deaf, such as a double tap on the rear for "sit."

Blind and deaf dogs **map** their surroundings using their paws. Changes in texture help them to "see" where they are. Carpet runners on the floor create a clear and safe path for a blind and deaf dog to follow.

GEAR

Put an "I'm blind" or "I'm deaf" collar or bandana on your dog to let others know. You can use a remotely controlled vibrating collar to get the attention of a deaf dog. Instead of a clicker (page 112), a flashlight can be used as a reward marker for deaf dogs.

**MEET
KATHERINE S. &
KOOPER
OWNER OF BLIND
AND DEAF DOG**

"It can be a monumental challenge to care for a blind and deaf dog, but I choose to focus on the gifts Kooper has to offer. I am inspired by how he doesn't let any perceived obstacle prevent him from living a normal dog life. Kooper is currently working on his therapy dog certification, so he can cheer and inspire others.

KATHERINE'S TIP: "Your dog will appreciate safe, fun dogs toys, such as ones that dispense treats or wiggle. Let your dog know you are leaving with a special gesture, such as four pats on the chest, so your dog won't walk around the house searching for you."

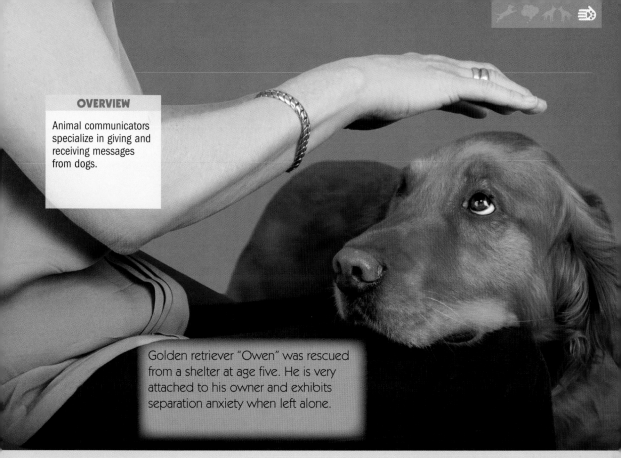

Animal communicators specialize in giving and receiving messages from dogs.

Golden retriever "Owen" was rescued from a shelter at age five. He is very attached to his owner and exhibits separation anxiety when left alone.

Animal Communicator

Whether you have a specific communication problem with your dog that you'd like to explore or just for fun, you can have your dog's thoughts read by an animal communicator. **Animal psychologists** or **pet whisperers** use their knowledge of animal body language and behavior to communicate with a dog.

Pet psychics claim to communicate psychically with animals via the animal's electromagnetic energy, similar to reiki and therapeutic touch healing. Some communicate with animals who are far away, via the telephone or by looking at a photograph of the animal. Some even communicate with deceased animals.

HOW TO GET STARTED

Animal communicators are often at dog shows or fairs and will do a 10-minute reading on your dog.

MEET DR. ISABELLE ANNETTE SCHMID, DVM, PH.D.
ANIMAL COMMUNICATOR, REINACH, SWITZERLAND

"I am trained in traditional Chinese medicine for animals and learned to communicate with animals. One client of mine had rescued an Appenzeller Sennenhund [Swiss herding dog] who hated being left alone in her apartment. The dog told me that he had once been left alone in an apartment which caught fire. Several weeks later my client was in the village from where the dog was adopted. A villager stopped her on the street asking if this was the dog who was rescued from a local apartment fire."

ISABELLE'S TIP: "Die Liebe ist das Yang im Yin der Stille [Love is Yang in the stillness of Yin.]"

OVERVIEW

Socialize your puppy,
build her confidence,
and teach her basic
manners and behaviors.

This seven-week-old
Australian shepherd
puppy attends puppy
class where she learns
to wear a collar, explore
a tunnel, and play with
other puppies.

Puppy Class

The first five months of a puppy's life are a critical socialization period. During this time your puppy should have as many positive new experiences as possible: take her places; let her meet lots of people and animals; and expose her to noise, different and unstable surfaces, and new challenges. With early, positive exposure your puppy learns to be at ease around people and other dogs and will become a more confident and stable dog.

Puppy classes are an opportunity to let your young pup interact with other puppies of a similar age. Often puppy classed will provide agility equipment (page 12) to challenge the puppies and socialize them to new and strange apparatus. Classes generally focus on: socialization; relationship-building; puppy health tips, grooming, and nutrition; basic manners and bite inhibition; and introduction to simple behaviors, such as sit, down, come, stay, walk on a loose leash, leave it, and settle. Puppies are taught with positive reinforcement methods, which involve lots of praise and food treats.

A kennel club **puppy certification program** (such as AKC's S.T.A.R. Puppy program) offers a goal for puppy early achievers. A certified evaluator evaluates you and your puppy on tests such as allowing you to put a collar on her, to hug her, and to take a toy away from her. She must know the beginnings of the sit, down, and come commands.

GEAR

Puppies should wear a flat collar and never a choke chain (slip chain) or prong collar.

HOW TO GET STARTED

An important early skill for puppies is the **settle** behavior. Pick your puppy up facing you and slowly roll her back onto your extended legs. Stroke her gently and say "settle" in a soft, pleasant voice.

Gently keep her on her back until she relaxes. Once she relaxes, relax your hold on her. Require only a few seconds of calmness before releasing her. Do not release your puppy while she is squirming, or you will be teaching her that she gets release from fighting you. Release her only when she is calm.

MEET MOLLY FEENEY & TALULAH
OWNER, "JUST PAWS PUPPY TRAINING"

"At 5 months, my Carolina dog/ Shiba Inu mix, Talulah, went for spay surgery and nearly died from septicemia and was in the ICU for a week. While recovering, she could not socialize for two months. This lack of socialization during her critical developmental window caused her to have fear and anxiety with new people and to shut down completely in new environments.

"I brought Talulah with me every place I could and helped her to become resocialized by making each new experience a positive one. Today Talulah is a happy, social dog amongst all dogs. She's still a little shy with new people initially, but once she gets a good sniff and a treat, she'll brush her entire body up against them asking to be pet."

MOLLY'S TIP: "Socialize your puppy right away! Your new puppy should meet, smell, see, and have positive interactions with 100 new things in one month, starting from the day you bring him or her home."

IDEAL DOGS FOR THIS ACTIVITY:

Puppy classes welcome puppies eight weeks to six months of age. Puppy obedience classes accept puppies up to two years of age and include frequent breaks.

German shepherd dog "Mona" proudly wears a backpack displaying her Canine Good Citizen patch.

Canine Good Citizen

Canine Good Citizen (CGC) certification programs (also called **Good Citizen Dog**, **Canine Good Neighbour**, or similar) acknowledges dogs that can demonstrate good manners in the community. Some therapy dog groups (page 178) require a CGC certification, and some youth citizenship groups (page 126) use this model as a beginning dog training program for children. Some hotels will only accept dog guests who are CGC certified.

To earn their CGC certification, the dog and owner must pass a series of tests administered by a certified evaluator. Tests include: polite interaction with a stranger; petting by a stranger; accepting grooming; walking on a loose leash; walking through a crowd; sit, down, stay; come when called; reaction to another dog; reaction to a large or noisy distraction; and supervised separation from owner. Owners may use praise and encouragement throughout the test and may pet their dog between exercises. Food treats and toys are not permitted during testing. The dog must pass all of the tests in order to pass. A dog that growls, snaps, bites, or attempts to attack a person or another dog is not a good citizen and will be dismissed from the test.

GEAR

All tests are performed on leash. Dogs should wear well-fitting buckle or slip collars made of leather, fabric, or chain. Special training collars such as prong collars and head halters are not permitted during the test. Upon passing the test, your dog will receive a certificate and you can purchase a medal or patch for him to wear.

HOW TO GET STARTED

This certification is offered by kennel clubs worldwide. Certified evaluators can test you and your dog. Tests are often administered at pet events. Some dog training schools offer a specific class that prepares you and your dog for this goal.

MEET COURTNEY HUTHER & SASSY
CANINE GOOD CITIZENS

"An eight week old German-shepherd/Rottweiler puppy was left at the shelter where I volunteer. The puppy didn't like to be held and showed aggression (she guarded her food bowl and even bit a kennel worker). Because she failed her temperament test, the shelter was going to put her down. I fell in love with Sassy and fostered her for three months and then adopted her.

"After a lot of work, Sassy earned her S.T.A.R. Puppy medal and then her Canine Good Citizen certificate at eight months of age. I was so proud of her! Sassy later went on to get her Rally-O title."

COURTNEY'S TIP: "Your dog is never too young or too old to learn good manners, and having a goal of getting your certificate will keep you motivated to train."

IDEAL DOGS FOR THIS ACTIVITY:

Any dog can qualify for this certification. This is often the first step toward future competitive sports for a dog, such as Rally-o or agility.

THE DOG DISPLAYS POLITE AND CONTROLLED REACTION TO ANOTHER DOG

A proud 4-H program member hugs her golden retriever after earning a ribbon in the dog show.

Youth Dog Project

Worldwide youth organizations such as 4-H develop citizenship, leadership, and life skills through experiential learning programs. The educational philosophy of "learning by doing" encourages young people to be involved in their learning by doing, reflecting, and then applying their knowledge. Some of these programs began with an agricultural emphasis, teaching children about farm animals and rural living, and this remains a key focus for many groups.

Clubs are organized at the local level, and clubs can compete with their projects in contests at the local, state, regional, or national levels.

Local clubs usually focus on one or more topics of the members' choice. They conduct project-related activities, such as a **dog project** where kids learn about: dog anatomy; how to feed, care for, and keep a dog healthy; grooming, fitting, and training practices; appreciation for dogs' places in society; responsibility as a dog owner; and dog-related careers. With the help of trainers, kids train their own dogs and compete with them at a fair in events such as **showmanship**, **obedience**, **tricks** contests, or dog **costume** contests.

HOW TO GET STARTED

Youth organizations such as 4-H exist in more than 80 countries around the world. Youth can become involved by joining a club, attending a camp, or joining a school-based or after-school program.

Many colleges and universities have collegiate clubs that support the youth service programs by serving as judges and conducting training workshops.

The worldwide community also includes over a half-million volunteers. If you have skills as a dog trainer or in another dog-related area, serve the youth of your community by volunteering as a dog project leader or by lending hands-on help during their training meetings.

MEET ANNA WEILBACHER (AGE 12)
WINNER, 4-H DOG TRICKS, CALIFORNIA

"I've been doing the dog project since I was 9 and I compete in showmanship, obedience, and tricks. When I started teaching tricks to Cookie my family couldn't believe the things I taught her! She can shake hands, say her prayers, go sit on a chair, and she can even play the shell game where she tells me which cup is hiding her ball."

ANNA'S TIP: "Feed your dog yourself and don't have your mom do it. That way your dog will pay more attention to you. And use cheese and hot dogs for training treats."

MEET JUSTIN MILLER (AGE 12)
WINNER, 4-H SHOWMANSHIP, CALIFORNIA

"Earl started out as a family dog, but now he is definitely *my* dog. Earl is a beagle. I had been told that beagles aren't the easiest dogs to train, but I never gave up on him. When we won showmanship this year I was so proud of him!"

JUSTIN'S TIP: "Start with the basics like teaching sit, down, and stay, before you go on to other stuff."

IDEAL DOGS FOR THIS ACTIVITY:

Youth programs emphasize caring for an animal and knowledge of an animal, and kids are encouraged to make the most of the dog they already own.

Briard "Henry" looks attentively at his owner during a rally obedience trial.

90°
Pivot
Right

Rally-O

Rally-o (also called **rally obedience** or **rally**) is a quickly growing competition obedience dog sport. Dog and handler teams navigate a course of ten to twenty numbered stations, each with a sign indicating a behavior to perform at that station such as "halt and sit," "U-turn," "moving down," or "call dog front and finish left." This is a self-guided course in which the handler proceeds with her dog at heel, at her own pace, through each station.

Unlike traditional obedience (page 130), handlers are allowed to encourage, praise, and double command their dogs during the course. Some organizations even allow the dog to be rewarded with treats in the ring, although this is not the norm. Scoring is not as rigorous as traditional obedience, and perfect heel position is not required.

Rally is often a stepping stone from the Canine Good Citizen program (page 124) to the world of obedience or agility (page 12) competition. It offers both the dog and handler an experience that is fun and energizing. Rally was designed with the traditional pet owner in mind, but it can still be very challenging for those who enjoy higher levels of competition.

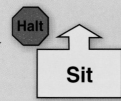

GEAR

Printable rally signs are available on the websites of the sanctioning clubs (see Resources section). Signs are placed so that the handler passes them on her right side.

HOW TO GET STARTED

In competition, you will be provided an opportunity to walk the rally course on your own, before the start of competition. Walk through once to learn the flow of the course. Walk through a second time to devise a handling strategy. Walk a third time exactly as you plan to do it with your dog (including giving commands and signals to your invisible dog, as well as praise and reward).

MEET SHIRLEY INDELICATO & RASCAL & MONTY
COMPETITION RALLY-O JUDGE

"I trained my first dog in 1945. He was a miniature poodle named Poko (but I called him the dog from hell!). He would race through the house and bark and snap at the toilet. I bought a dog book, and I would read a few pages, and then go out and work him, and read a few more pages, and work him again.

"Methods have changed through the years, and today we use much more positive reinforcement in training (although discipline is still necessary).

"Monty was my first rally dog. I put an obedience UD [Utility title] on him before we started rally. He transitioned very easily and really enjoyed rally.

"My older mini poodle, Denise, was retired from competition, but she still wanted to work. Rally was perfect for her, because it gave her a job but allowed me to be close to her and give her that extra encouragement."

SHIRLEY'S TIP: "Nerves travel down the leash. Take three deep breaths before you enter the ring."

IDEAL DOGS FOR THIS SPORT:

Dogs of all ages and breeds can excel at Rally-O. This sport is great for dogs that are less confident and appreciate the praise from their handler as they work.

In an impressive demonstration of training, the owner handles his dog through a rigid series of competition exercises.

A golden retriever performs the "retrieve over high jump" exercise as part of his open-level obedience trial.

Obedience Competition

Dog obedience is a competition sport in which you and your dog work as a team to earn titles and rankings. Each competition level is tested at a **trial** and consists of six or seven defined exercises that are performed in a ring and scored by a judge.

Novice level exercises consist of things like **on-leash heeling**, **heel free** (off-leash), **figure-8 heeling**, **recall** (come), **stand for examination**, **sit-stay**, and **down-stay** (stays are done with the handler at the opposite end of the ring).

More advanced competition levels consist of exercises such as **retrieving a dumbbell over a high jump** (see photo at left), **drop on recall** (handler commands the dog to lie down in the middle of a recall), and **5 minute stays** with the handler out of sight. Some of the top level exercises are a **signal exercise**, where the handler guides his dog using only hand signals and no voice commands, and **scent discrimination**, where the dog must find the one article within a pile of identical articles that has his owner's scent.

While the exercises themselves may not sound overly difficult, they become much more challenging in the competition ring: the handler cannot use food treats; may not correct his dog, guide his dog, nor touch his dog's collar; and can give no more than one command for each behavior.

GEAR

The dog wears a flat or chain collar in the ring and may not wear a prong or martingale collar. Short leather leads are commonly used. Because competitors wear an armband in the ring, trainers sometimes train with an armband which holds treats. That way, in the ring, your dog will think you have treats!

HOW TO GET STARTED

Practice matches are organized to feel just like a trial but are not official, and allow the trainer to reward or correct his dog in the ring. Experienced competition dogs sometimes become **ringwise**, knowing that they won't be corrected or rewarded during a competition, and practice matches allow the trainer to break this habit.

MEET DENNIS BETTS & BOO HIGH-IN-TRIAL OBEDIENCE CHAMPIONS

"I wanted Boo to be my hunting companion—but she was afraid of the water and the scary duck decoys and had little interest in retrieving.

"I started her in obedience classes to improve her social skills and help her gain confidence. Boo was very proud of her new skills and her personality and desire to please blossomed! This confidence carried over into retrieving where she learned to work through her fears. Boo went on to become one of only 16 female Goldens to achieve both an OTCH [obedience champion title] and a Master Hunter title. When Boo does well in an obedience competition, we stop on the way home for a cheeseburger—her favorite!"

DENNIS' TIP: "Many men don't give enough praise in their training. A sing-songy voice is instinctively rewarding to your dog. Sometimes you've got to be silly in order to make your dog happy."

IDEAL DOGS FOR THIS SPORT:

All breeds are capable of passing obedience competition levels, but the dogs that earn the blue ribbons are generally quick, high energy dogs such as border collies and golden retrievers. They get the extra points for style as they bounce quickly into position.

OVERVIEW

Protection sports test the dog's ability to protect himself and his handler. Trials are similar to the work performed by police dogs.

A Belgian Malinois grips the bite sleeve of the decoy during a training exercise.

Schutzhund

Schutzhund (meaning **protection dog**), also called **versatility dog**, tests a dog for the traits necessary for police-type work such as police K-9, odor/drug detection (page 78), tracking, and search and rescue (page 86). The dog must demonstrate courage, intelligence, trainability, and a desire to work, as well as physical strength, endurance, agility, and scenting ability. Schutzhund **trials** (tests) consists of three phases: **tracking** (page 82), **obedience** (page 130), and **protection**. Through trials, dogs earn levels of schutzhund titles.

In the protection phase of the test, a **decoy** person is used to test the dog's courage in protecting himself and his handler and to test his ability to be controlled while doing so. The decoy, wearing a heavily padded **bite sleeve** on one arm, hides behind one of several identical blinds. The dog searches the blinds and barks to indicate when he has found the decoy. The dog then guards the decoy to prevent him from moving. In an exercise similar to police work, the handler searches the decoy and transports him to the judge. During this process the decoy either attacks the dog or the handler or attempts to escape. The dog must stop the attack or the escape by biting the bite sleeve. When the attack or escape stops, the dog is commanded to "out" (release the sleeve.) The dog must show both courage and obedience while in this state of high drive.

GEAR

Tug toys are heavily used to reward a dog during protection training. Working police dogs and search and rescue dogs are rewarded with a good game of tug with a jute stick or Kong on a rope.

HOW TO GET STARTED

Before he can enter a Schutzhund competition, a dog must first pass a temperament test called a **Begleithundprüfung** (**B** or **BH**). This tests his basic obedience as well as his sureness around strange people, dogs, traffic, and loud noises (such as gunshots).

The majority of Schutzhund training is done by owners at local clubs. Before joining a club, watch one of their training sessions and ask questions about their training methods. Training should be reward-based and focused on control and not aggression. See the following pages to learn how to teach your dog to guard and object.

MEET TIM WILMOTH & KIMON
VON DER WILMOTHHAUS KENNEL;
K-9 HANDLER;
SCHUTZHUND COMPETITOR

"My nitrate detection (bomb sniffing) K-9's performed numerous security sweeps for high profile dignitaries. During one such sweep with my German shepherd Eiche, former British Prime Minister Margaret Thatcher bent down to pet him, 'What a wonderful Alsation! These dogs keep me alive.' As she walked away she suddenly turned back, 'Eiche, I am on my way to my VIP reception. I invite you to come!' She grinned and looked at me and said, 'Since you are on the end of the leash you may attend, too!'

"Having worked Police K-9s for many years, I didn't see the use for schutzhund with my dogs. I was wrong. Schutzhund complements my police and scent dogs. Kimon is my Patrol/Narcotics K-9. He is 6 times Schutzhund Sch3, Koerklasse 1 for life. I have experienced 'all worlds' of the dog: I have trialed them on the trial field, shown them in the ring, worked them on the street, and had them as my loyal companions."

TIM'S TIP: "Surround yourself with people who are willing to share their knowledge and don't be intimidated by the sport. Schutzhund is a sport anyone can enjoy!"

IDEAL DOGS FOR THIS SPORT:

Dogs of any breed, even mixes, can compete in Schutzhund today, but the most common breeds are German shepherd dogs, Belgian Malinois, Rottweilers, Dobermans, giant schnauzers, Bouvier des Flandres, beaucerons, American bulldogs, boxers, Airedale terriers, and the like.

A schutzhund **Wachthunde** (or watch dog) certificate includes an **object guard** test.

OBJECT GUARD:

In an **object guard** exercise the handler asks her dog to guard an object (such as a briefcase, stroller, or bicycle) and then leaves the dog. The dog is trained to stay touching the object and to bark at anyone who approaches it. For police work, this skill is taught with aggression; however, in sport it is taught as a cued behavior. The steps below show you how to teach your dog to stay with the object, but do not instruct on the aggression that would follow if a thief approached. In the vast majority of cases, a dog standing near an object would be enough to deter theft.

1 It will be easiest for your dog to understand to stand on an object (such as a suitcase) rather than to stay near an object (such as a bicycle). Start with a large object that your dog can stand on or put his front paws on. Cue "on guard" and use a food treat to lure your dog on top. Release the treat once he is on top.

2 Command your dog to "stay" and hold up your palm. After a few seconds, give him another treat (give the treat while he is still on the object).

3 Add distance and duration by backing up farther and having your dog hold his stay longer. Walk around him in a circle. Your dog will naturally turn to face you, and this is fine. If your dog leaves the object, immediately instruct him back on the object, but do not give him a treat. Have him guard the object a short time and then go back and reward him.

4 Have a **decoy** (person representing a potential thief) move in and try to pull the suitcase a little. If your dog jumps off or falls off, immediately tell him "on guard" and have him step back up.

WHAT TO EXPECT: Dogs can become confused when the decoy enters the training. Use an instructive and enthusiastic tone with your dog rather than a reprimanding one.

TIP: Always give your dog a treat when you return to him. That's his payment for his job!

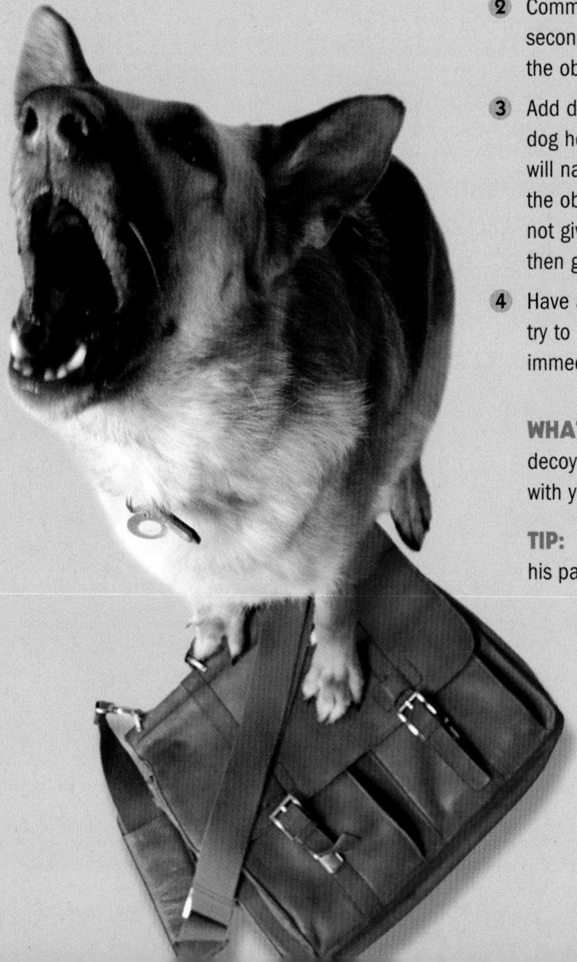

1 Use a treat to lure your dog onto a large object. Release the treat when his paws are on top.

2 Have your dog "stay" on the object for a few seconds and then give him a treat.

3 Walk around your dog and encourage him to watch you but not take his paws off the object.

4 Have a decoy try to take the object. Encourage your dog to stay on top.

In a wonderful display
of teamwork, dogs
are directed by their
handler to move sheep
through fences or
enclosures.

A sheep dog rounds up sheep during
the International Sheep Dog Trials
in Penrith, England. Top handlers
from England, Ireland, Scotland, and
Wales compete in front of crowds
for the fifteen places in the Supreme
Championship at Lowther Estate,
Cumbria.

Herding

Herding breed dogs were bred to help control the movement of sheep, cattle, and geese on farms and ranches. Today herding is a popular competition dog sport which relies heavily upon teamwork. Handlers use whistles and verbal commands such as "**come bye**" and "**away to me**" to send their dog clockwise or counterclockwise around the herd.

Noncompetitive **herding tests** and competitive **herding trials** (also called **sheepdog trials**) are simulations of pastoral or farm tasks in which a handler directs one or two dogs to move three to six sheep around a field, fences, gates, or enclosures. Competitors are scored by time and obedience and penalized if a sheep strays from the course.

In one type of herding event the dogs must split six sheep into two groups of three and then conduct each group through a defined course and into pens. The **heading dog** gathers and moves one group of sheep while the other group is guarded by the **eye dog** (who holds the sheep still by his head movement). This event is difficult because sheep always want to stay together in one group.

GEAR

Semicircle or triangle herding dog whistles are used to communicate commands to the working dog (see page 110). Handlers carry a **crook** or **stock stick**, which is used in practical herding to hook a sheep's neck to catch for shearing or doctoring. In sport herding, the stick is used to guide or signal the dog while working the sheep.

HOW TO GET STARTED

A herding instructor can give your dog a herding **instinct test** to reveal your dog's drive, style, strengths, and weaknesses. Your dog needs no prior training for an instinct test. The instructor will be looking for his ability to move and control two or three sheep by **fetching** or **driving** them in a round pen. The trainer may put his own well-trained dog in the pen as well to give your dog the idea what to do.

MEET TERRY KENNEY & ROBBER
TRIPLE CHAMPION, TRIAL JUDGE

"I bought my first herding dog, a border collie, as a gift for my wife. At the time we lived next door to a riding club that did cattle roping, cutting, and team penning. After seven months of my dog chasing the cattle and wrecking havoc at the club, I was politely (and firmly) asked to either 'learn to utilize my dog's god-given instinct or to keep her the **** off of the grounds'. That threat not only started me in the sport of herding; it changed the course of my life."

TERRY'S TIP: "An untrained dog can create enough work for 20 cowboys, but a trained dog can do the work of 20 cowboys (and with no back talk!). Remember that your dog was born with a herding instinct. You probably were not. Learn to trust your dog."

IDEAL DOGS FOR THIS SPORT:

Primarily herding breeds compete, although some organizations allow any dog that has been trained to work stock. Popular herding breeds are border collie, German shepherd dog, Shetland sheepdog, rough collie, old English sheepdog, and bearded collie.

Herding breeds are divided into **eye breeds** (border collie and kelpie) which crouch and use their stare to intimidate the sheep, and **upright breeds**, who use their presence to work sheep.

Dogs and their professional or volunteer handlers are used to chase nuisance geese from parks, golf courses, and airports.

Border collie "Kit" works to move a goose from a body of water at a cemetery. The dogs don't chase the nuisance geese but harass them into flight and away from the grounds that they are clearing.

Geese Wrangler

An abundance of geese can be an nuisance at parks and golf courses, leaving droppings and acting aggressively toward people. At airports, ducks and geese are large enough to pose a real danger to planes. Rather than kill the birds, specially trained geese wrangler dogs are employed across the country to chase them away.

Border collies are the most common breed used as geese wranglers, as they are said to be able to hypnotize herd animals with their stare. They don't chase or bite the geese, but rather they put their head down, their tail between their legs, and stalk the geese. Dogs are sent out individually or more commonly in pairs. They will chase the birds into the air or the water and keep them from getting back on land to feed. Perpetual harassment of the birds will prevent their courtship and nesting behavior and force the birds to move on.

Bird harassment programs are generally long-term projects and must be maintained. Once the dog goes away, the birds will return soon thereafter, sometimes the very same day. To be effective, dogs must work the site every day and sometimes several times per day.

Professional geese wranglers may be contracted to patrol places where geese are causing problems. Volunteer dog patrols can be organized within a community to patrol their local parks.

GEAR

Dogs wear a vest while they are working. If they are expected to swim after geese, they should wear a buoyancy vest.

HOW TO GET STARTED

Because geese wrangler dogs will be off-leash and may come into contact with other people or dogs, many trainers choose to get their Canine Good Citizen certificate (page 124).

Dogs typically train for 12 to 16 months, practicing on Indian Runner ducks, which do not fly and are not very fearful of dogs. Dogs learn to stalk the ducks but not hurt them.

MEET DAVID C. MARCKS & GAIL
FOUNDER, GEESE POLICE

"My company, Geese Police, was the pioneer of this industry. I gave up my civil service career to go into geese policing because I love being outside working with my dogs (much more fun than being inside doing paperwork!).

"I use my specially training working border collies to rid areas of Canada geese. They love their work and can't wait to get started every day."

DAVID'S TIP: "Not every border collie is slated for goose control work. This doesn't mean it's a bad dog, it just means it needs different work."

IDEAL DOGS FOR THIS ACTIVITY:

Herding breeds excel at this work because they have both the prey drive and the herding instinct. Border collies and kelpies are known for their ability to crouch and control a herd with their eye and are especially effective. Hunting or retrieving breeds are not used for the safety of the geese.

Trained dogs in obedience class hold their sit-stays, even while the instructor proofs them by using a toy to try to tempt them forward. The dog owners stand behind their dogs, ready to correct them if they break their stay.

Dog Trainer

Dog trainer is a generic term that applies to a variety of dog training specialists. **Animal behaviorists** read a dog's body language to analyze behavior problems. They specialize in resolving common behavior problems such as aggression, separation anxiety, destructive behavior, barking, jumping, and inconsistent recall. Behaviorists emphasize behavior modification through positive training techniques.

Pet dog trainers teach manners and basic obedience skills to dogs and teach their owners dog training skills. Specialized **sport trainers** instruct owners and their dogs in competition sports such as agility, musical canine freestyle, or rally obedience. **Working dog trainers** train dogs for jobs such as guide dogs, hunting dogs, herding dogs, police dogs, search and rescue dogs, and animal actors.

Today's methods of dog training rely upon operant conditioning methods that focus primarily on **positive reinforcement** and repetition. New behaviors are taught through five strategies: luring, molding, mimicking, capturing, and shaping. Unwanted behaviors are reduced primarily through a strategy of penalizing the dog by taking away a desired thing as a consequence. For example, if your dog jumps on you, you would turn away and remove your attention as a consequence for that undesired behavior.

GEAR

A dog trainer uses a **bait bag** at her waist, a short leash, and perhaps a **target stick** and a **clicker** (page 112).

HOW TO GET STARTED

Different trainers will use different methods. Audit a training class before signing up, and talk to the trainer about her motivational strategies as well as her use of corrections. If at any time during a training class you are not comfortable with the methods being used on your dog, you need to intervene.

If you are interested in becoming a dog trainer yourself, several schools offer programs, both on site and remotely (see Resources, page 202). A good trainer will have a combination of book knowledge and hands-on experience. Gain hands-on experience by volunteering to work with dogs at your animal shelter.

MEET IAN DUNBAR & CLAUDE & DUNE
FOUNDER: ASSOC. OF PET DOG TRAINERS (APDT); DOGSTARDAILY.COM

"In 1981 I set out to teach the world's first off-leash puppy socialization and training class. I remember thinking 'I've never trained a dog in my life!' But I just did what came naturally; I employed the lure/reward training techniques that my father and grandfather used with their farm animals and gundogs. That, combined with behavioral science, and the puppies in the class quickly learned what we wanted. But more importantly, they learned to *want* to do it. Thus, a new field of *pet* dog training was whelped and the SIRIUS® Puppy Training video spread the word about science-based dog training. In 1994 progressive trainers came together with the formation of the Association of Pet Dog Trainers (APDT), which developed the first international Certification Program for Dog Trainers (CPDT)."

MEET PATRICIA McCONNELL, PH.D. & WILL
CERTIFIED APPLIED ANIMAL BEHAVIORIST

"My favorite part of being a behaviorist and trainer is working with my two favorite species: people and dogs. I love them both, quirky and silly as we both are. It's a joy to act as a bridge between individuals of different species, who sometimes communicate deeply and profoundly, and yet who sometimes miscommunicate and misunderstand one another. Professionally, I am fascinated by the close bond between us and our four-legged friends. It's a biological miracle that we love dogs so much and that they love us equally, and it's something that we should celebrate."

Dog and handler perform a creative and original choreographed dance to music, showcasing teamwork, synchronization, artistry, costuming, and style.

Mary Ray performs Heelwork to Music to the theme of Riverdance at the Crufts Dog Show. Mary Ray is the founder of this sport, having first demonstrated it in the early 1990s.

Musical Canine Freestyle

Musical canine freestyle (also called **dog dancing**) is a mixture of dog obedience, tricks, and dance that showcases creative interaction and the bond between a dog and her owner.

Dog dancing has two competition variations, both scored on technical and artistic merit. **Freestyle heeling** (also known as **heelwork to music**) focuses on a dog's ability to stay in variations of the heel position (including heeling on the handler's right side as well as the traditional left side) while the handler moves to music. Pivots, forward, backward, and diagonal moves are important to the routine. **Musical freestyle** is a showy form of competition showcasing dance ability, creativity, and innovative dog tricks which complement the owner's dance moves. Moves may include leg weaves, figure-8s through the handler's legs, jumps, spins, bows, rolls, and leg kicks.

Exhibition freestyle is a no-holds-barred routine designed to demonstrate the full extent of creativity and excitement that musical freestyle can offer. Highly entertaining and drawing huge crowds, it allows for moves, props, cues, and costumes that would not always be allowed on the competition circuit.

GEAR

Except in some beginner categories, training aids such as leashes and treats are not allowed in competition. Coordinating costumes for yourself and your dog should reflect your music. Props should be integral to the theme of the dance, and may include hoops (page 34) and variations of batons such as brooms or swords (page 38).

HOW TO GET STARTED

Routines often have a theme, such as a fairy tale, a gladiator fight, surfing, or a comedy routine. Choice of music and the way the routine reflects the music is important. Select a short musical piece (a minute or two) that reflects your dog's attitude and pace (chose a tempo that matches your dog's energy level). Choreograph a routine and break it into pieces of two or three moves. Train these pieces as a sequence.

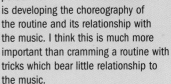

MEET MARY RAY
ORIGINATOR OF HEELWORK TO MUSIC

"I love music. My favorite part of HTM is developing the choreography of the routine and its relationship with the music. I think this is much more important than cramming a routine with tricks which bear little relationship to the music.

"I don't limit myself to what has been done before. I'll incorporate multiple dogs in my exhibitions and props and even dancers."

MARY'S TIP: "Some moves may be more difficult for certain breeds or dogs. Make sure that your dog is comfortable with what you are asking him to do. Because there are no compulsory moves, there is no need to do anything that you or your dog are not happy with. You can build your routine to suit the things that you and your dog enjoy and do best."

IDEAL DOGS FOR THIS SPORT:

Every breed of dog can excel at dog dancing, but the trick is for the trainer to choose music and a routine which play to her dog's strengths. Some of the top dogs have been border collies, golden retrievers, poodles, and various mixed breeds.

OVERVIEW

Synchronized heeling and formation marching come together in an impressive exhibition.

The Southern Golden Retriever Display Team performs a synchronized routine at the Crufts Dog Show. All of the dogs on the team must have their U.K. Kennel Club Good Citizen Dog Scheme Gold Award (see page 124).

K-9 Drill Team

If you are looking for a noncompetitive group activity to do with your dog and your dog-loving friends, K-9 drill team might be for you. K-9 drill team (also called **display team**) is an exhibition sport combining heeling and formation marching. Teams perform in parades, at dog shows, and at sporting events.

There are no rules, regulations, or defined ways to perform, so each team may choose to interpret the sport. You are limited only by your imagination!

There are generally eight to sixteen owners, each handling one dog. The dogs walk at heel while the owners march in formation patterns such as circles, spirals, weaves, and serpentine maneuvers. Some teams chose to incorporate props such as flags, dog tricks, or dance steps. Some teams have a routine performed in time to music (similar to musical canine freestyle, page 142).

Other teams learn elements and use a **drillmaster** to call them out. This format works well for parade performances, when the team needs to have both moving and stationary patterns. Simple elements may include right turn, left turn, U turn, and halt and sit. Complex elements may include having the group form concentric circles (small and slow dogs on the inside) and forming two parallel lines which cross and switch places. The drillmaster first calls the element, waits a few seconds for the team to prepare, and then whistles to cue the team to perform the element in unison.

GEAR

Costumes or uniforms greatly add to the synchronized effect. If your team chooses to work off-leash, a short tab lead attached to the dog's collar will give you quick control when you need it.

HOW TO GET STARTED

Your dog will need to know basic obedience, such as walking at heel, sit, and stay. With your group, plan some formations on paper and assign them names. Practice them first on your own before involving your dogs.

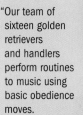

MEET KAREN MENTER & SAFFY
TEAM MANAGER, SOUTHERN GOLDEN RETRIEVER SOCIETY DISPLAY TEAM

"Our team of sixteen golden retrievers and handlers perform routines to music using basic obedience moves.

"The aim of the display is to show well-trained family pets having a good time with their handlers in a very entertaining way. The team performs at venues such as Crufts Dog Show, Discover Dogs in London, country fairs, village fetes, and for animal charities and hospices. "

KAREN'S TIP: "Make sure your dog understands what you want. Make everything fun for your dog and he will want to please you. Our dogs think they belong to a doggy youth club!"

IDEAL DOGS FOR THIS ACTIVITY:

Dogs of any shape, size, and breeding can enjoy K-9 drill team! Dogs must be well socialized and not aggressive toward other dogs. Since you may perform at a fair or parade, your dog should be accustomed to distractions of noises, people, and smells.

Standard poodle "Donny" (UK & Am CH Afterglow The Big Tease) gaits around the ring at the international championship Crufts Dog Show in Birmingham, England. Crufts is the world's largest and most prestigious dog show, with more than 22,000 dogs competing. Donny was the 2008 top winning dog of all breeds in Britain.

Conformation Dog Show

The most popular form of canine competition is the conformation dog show (also referred to as **breed show**, or **ringcraft**). The dog is judged on his **conformation** (overall appearance and structure). Every breed has a recognized **breed standard** representing its ideal characteristics. A dog show judge compares each dog to his breed standard to find the dog nearest to that ideal.

The judge evaluates the dog on his **appearance**, **movement**, and **temperament**. Dogs are lined up and **stacked** (positioned squarely and evenly so that the judge can evaluate their structure) and then **gaited** (run) around the ring. Unlike almost every other form of dog sport competition, food treats are allowed in the conformation ring and are used to **bait** the dog and get an alert expression.

Competitions consist of several rounds, beginning with dogs of the same breed competing against each other (initially **dog** and **bitch** classes are split) to vie for **Best of Breed** (BOB). Breed winners compete against the other breed winners within their **breed group** (a group being: terriers, hounds, toys, etc.). Finally the seven **group winners** come together to compete for the top title of **Best in Show** (BIS). When a dog has achieved the necessary number of competition points, the dog is said to have **finished** and has the prefix of **champion** (abbreviated CH) added to his name.

GEAR

Conformation leads are delicate, barely visible, and intended to sit high and tight around the dog's neck to keep his head held high. **Martingale** leads (also known as **limited slip**) are all-in-one collars and leads with a tight plastic bead which slides down the lead to keep the collar in place. Chain collars are used for larger breeds.

Handlers are smartly dressed, often in suits and ties for the gentlemen and skirt suits and flats for the ladies. Your outfit should stand out from the color of your dog and not be distracting (you want the judge's eyes on your dog and not on you).

HOW TO GET STARTED

Handling classes will prepare you for the ring. See page 149 for some tips on stacking your dog. Some owners choose to hire a professional handler in the ring.

MEET MICHAEL GADSBY & DONNY
BREEDER, HANDLER, OWNER

"In heavily-coated breeds like poodles, presentation is a high priority, and keeping a dog's skin and coat in peak form is an integral part of success. Despite Donny's pristine appearance in the show ring, he lives his day to day life as a 'normal' dog, playing outside and get dirty. This lifestyle is essential for a show dog to perform with the exuberance and energy that we desire."

MICHAEL'S TIP: "Whether you are new to showing dogs or a seasoned pro, never take the basics for granted. Strive to make your dogs look and feel their best. Maybe that means taking them for a run even though you don't feel like going out or giving a dog an extra bath to keep his coat in top condition on a night when you'd rather watch the telly. Dogs benefit from the attention you give them and doing the proper groundwork puts you one step ahead when you enter the ring each weekend."

IDEAL DOGS FOR THIS SPORT:

Conformation dog shows are limited to purebred dogs who are registered with an eligible sanctioning organization such as the American Kennel Club (AKC) or The Kennel Club (in the United Kingdom). Dogs must be intact (not spayed or neutered).

OVERVIEW

Mixed-breed dogs are the stars of these shows, competing in a variety of fun categories.

Mixed-breed dogs compete at the annual 'Nuts for Mutts' celebrity judged companion dog show in Los Angeles, California. This televised show raises funds for animal rescue. Competition categories include fastest mutt, most ear-resistible ears, best smile, best trick, and best kisser.

Companion Dog Show

Dog shows (page 146) are no longer just for purebreeds! A number of fun competitions have arisen to give mutts a chance to shine. In some, such as the **Companion Dog Club** offered by The Kennel Club (UK), handlers are judged on their exhibiting (ringcraft) skills. Handlers stack, bait, and gait their mutt just as they would a purebred in a conformation dog show. Instead of the merits of the dogs being evaluated, it is the skill of the handlers that is judged.

Other companion dog shows offer fun categories to show off your dog's uniqueness. While purebreeds compete at Crufts Dog Show, mixed-breeds can compete at **Scruffts** for novelty titles such as most handsome dog, prettiest bitch, best rescue, and waggiest tail.

MEET CLAIRE DORÉ & DANA
BEST IN SHOW, NUTS FOR MUTTS

"I entered the 'Best Trick' contest with my Aussie mutt, Dana, on a whim. I'm a movie dog trainer so I had Dana show off some of her acting behaviors. We won! Then the winners of each category competed for Best In Show. I had no expectation of winning, which is probably why we were so relaxed and able to enjoy each other in the moment. Perhaps the judges liked that, because they declared us the winners! (I say 'us' loosely, as it was my wonderful Dana who really won!)."

CLAIRE'S TIP: "Enjoy the event with your dog and let the judges see the honest bond that you have together."

1 Place your dog's front feet first.

STACK YOUR DOG:

Teach your dog to **stack** or stand squarely and still for judging. His feet should be facing forward, with his front legs straight and under his shoulder blades. His rear legs should be vertical from the hock down. His head should be high, chest forward, and tail up (depending on breed). Small dogs are stacked on a table.

1 Control your dog's head, either by hooking your thumb under the top of his collar or by holding his muzzle or cheek. Lift his chest until his front feet are off the ground and then lower him slowly down. This will put his feet straight and at the correct width apart.

2 Adjust one back foot at a time by lifting from above the hock.

3 With a wiggly dog it is sometimes easier to teach them to stack by placing each foot on a correctly placed brick.

4 Use their collar to hold their head high and forward.

WHAT TO EXPECT: Stacking a dog is not as easy at it looks—for the handler or for the dog. A show dog should be trained on his ringwork several times per week.

TIP: Treats, or **bait**, can be used to hold the dog's attention and give him an alert look.

2 Adjust each back foot.

3 Practice by stacking your dog on bricks.

4 Hold his head high, forward, and straight.

Sussex spaniel "Edward" and his junior handler trot around the ring at the Young Kennel Club dog show held in conjunction with the Crufts benched dog show.

151b

Junior Handler

Through junior handler programs within established kennel clubs, children have the opportunity to compete in their age group at various dog events. These programs develop in children sportsmanship, a knowledge of dogs, familiarity with ring procedures and a bond between the child and her dog.

Junior showmanship is the most popular junior handler event. Children are divided into classes by age and experience, and are judged on how well they present their dogs. Unlike conformation dog shows (page 146), the quality of the dog's structure is not evaluated at all. Judging is based solely on the ringcraft skill of the child. The juniors move their dogs around the ring according to the judge's instructions. The judge notes whether the child presents the dog properly according to the dog's breed or type. In some shows, the children may be quizzed on their knowledge of dogs. The **Westminster Kennel Club** dog show in New York city is considered the crown jewel of junior showmanship.

Junior handlers may also compete in performance dog events such as obedience, agility, rally, tracking, hunting, and more. Although some organizations have separate categories for junior handlers in performance events, in most cases the child competes in the same ring as the adults. If the child qualifies, she earns the same titles and awards as adult handlers.

GEAR

The same gear that is used in the adult version of each sport is appropriate for the junior version.

HOW TO GET STARTED

Dogs naturally respond more readily to instruction from an adult than from a child. Adults have the advantage of size and a deeper voice, which conveys seriousness. If the child is to be respected and obeyed, then the child needs to be very involved in feeding the dog, training the dog, and rewarding the dog with play.

MEET ALEKSANDRA SZYDŁOWSKA & YORAM
LESZNO, POLAND.
WORLD DOG SHOW JUNIOR HANDLER OF THE YEAR, CRUFTS JUNIOR HANDLER OVER ALL WINNER

"I am 14 years old and have been showing dogs since I was 9. I used to be shy and scared of people. When my Borzoi, Yoram, came into my life he was also shy and scared of people. We helped each other. I started to be brave and to believe in myself. Yoram trusted me and I gave him my heart. Yoram is now gone, after a long illness, but I keep his photo in a necklace as my talisman.

"I now have six Borzois: Victory, Dudus, Josh, Amarok, Keyra, and Nanook."

ALEKSANDRA'S TIP: "The most important things are respect, and mutual trust with your dog. When you show, it is important to have a suitable but elegant look and appropriate hair style. It contributes to the general impression of the couple."

IDEAL DOGS FOR THIS SPORT:

Children may compete with dogs of any breed, however, the dog must meet the same eligibility requirements as in the adult version of the sport (such as being intact, registered, and purebred). Depending on the organization, the minimum age can be as young as two to nine years old.

Your dog can be a professional animal actor, starring in live shows, film, TV, and commercial shoots.

PRODUCTION_____

DIRECTOR_____

CAMERA_____

DATE   **SCENE**   **TAKE**

Four-year-old terrier mix "Iris" is a professional dog actor who has worked in movies, TV shows, and commercials. Iris was rescued from the shelter by a professional animal trainer who exposed her to many different people and situations to prepare her for acting. Iris can bark on cue, go to a mark, retrieve an object, beg, back up, cover her face with her paw, lower her head, wiggle on her back, and climb a ladder.

Animal Actor

Have you ever seen a dog in a movie and wondered if your pooch could become a pet star? Dog actors are used in movies, on TV, in commercials, and in live shows. Many dog actors are privately owned and contracted through **animal talent agencies**. The talent agency **preps** your dog by training him for the specific behaviors indicated in the script, and their **studio trainer** handles your dog on set.

A dog actor must be confident and well **socialized** to people, environments, and loud noises. He must be **set-trained** and able to perform basic **behaviors** on cue, such as sit, down, stand, on your side, come, stay, go to your mark, go with (an actor), back up, bark, hold an object, and watch. The dog must follow silent hand signal cues (page 114) when working on set. Certain verbal cues and hand signals are standard within the industry so that any studio trainer can work a set-trained dog. Most dog actors are **clicker trained** (page 112) for the same reason.

Professional animal actors are federally regulated to ensure they are treated humanely and not overworked. Private organizations such as the **American Humane Association** are hired on set to monitor the use of animals in the entertainment industry.

GEAR

Common set-training tools include a **bait stick** to direct the dog's gaze (see photo below), a **clicker**, a small disc to be used as a **mark**, a variety of toys and squeakers, yummy dog treats, peanut butter (to get a dog to sniff or lick something), a dog crate, and grooming brushes.

HOW TO GET STARTED

Submit photos of your dog along with his specifics (breed, size, and weight) and a list of behaviors that he performs reliably to an animal talent agency. Create a website for your dog that includes video clips. One of the first behaviors every set-trained dog actor learns is how to **go to a mark** (see the following pages for instruction).

MEET RAY BEAL & D.J.
PROFESSIONAL STUDIO ANIMAL TRAINER

"Siberian husky, D.J., played Demon in the *Snow Dogs* film and played Max in *Eight Below.* A movie set can be full of distractions, with animals, actors, and multiple trainers all giving cues to their animal at the same time. It's crazy! When I worked on the *Marley and Me* set, there were twenty-two yellow Labs acting as Marley. Each dog was prepped with different behaviors for different scenes."

RAY'S TIP: "Animal talent scouts frequently use the internet to scout dogs. Show off your dog's behaviors on a video. Show that your dog can perform behaviors at a distance from you."

IDEAL DOGS FOR THIS ACTIVITY:

Every breed of dog can be an animal actor, mixed breeds as well as purebreds. There is always demand for Labrador retrievers, golden retrievers, and scruffy terrier mutts. Unique looking breeds are also popular, including bloodhounds, standard poodles in show coat, Chinese cresteds, bulldogs, Great Danes, Chihuahuas, and shar peis. Light-colored dogs are generally preferred, as they are easier to light on camera.

An animal actor must be able to go to a mark on the set and stop there.

GO TO A MARK:

Start by teaching your dog to step on a large mark and eventually work toward a tiny piece of tape or small disc as the mark.

1 Choose at item to be your mark. It should be flat, so that your dog is not tempted to pick it up. Use tape to secure the mark onto a larger, study object. Use a food treat to lure your dog to place her front paws up on the mark.

2 As soon as her paws are on the mark, release the treat. Be sure to release the treat while she is in the correct position—with her paw on the mark.

3 Once your dog has the hang of that, step away a short distance, point to the mark, and say "go mark." The instant your dog's paws touch the mark, say "good!" to let her know that she just earned a treat. Follow up quickly with a treat.

4 Now put the mark on a smaller object, such as two bricks or a large book. Say "go mark" and once again use a treat to lure your dog onto it.

5 The instant she touches the mark with her paw, release the treat in your hand.

6 Once again, move a little away from the mark and send her to it with the cue "go mark!"

7 Put the mark on the floor. This time do not lure your dog onto it but rather just send her from a short distance. The moment she touches the mark, say "good!" and quickly follow up with a treat.

8 Gradually use smaller and smaller marks. On set your dog may have to find a mark no larger than a sticky note or a button.

WHAT TO EXPECT: Most dogs can learn the basics of this behavior in a week. If you are using a small mark or are in a new location, be sure to show your dog the mark and tap it with your finger to let her know where it is.

1. Affix a mark to a larger object and lure your dog onto it with a treat.

2. When her paws are on the mark, release the treat.

3. Send your dog to the mark from a short distance away.

4. Put the mark on a smaller object and lure your dog onto it.

5. Release the treat the moment she steps on the mark.

6. Cue your dog from a short distance to "go mark!"

7. Put the mark on the floor. Say "good!" the moment she touches it.

8. Use smaller and smaller marks.

OVERVIEW

Dog models are used in print shoots. Amateur dogs are commonly used, and cuteness counts in this activity!

A Yorkshire terrier models a stylish doggy coat at the 'Charli' dog fashion and grooming boutique in Moscow, Russia.

Moscow hosts a Russian Pet Fashion Week where designers display their canine couture to keep their haute hounds warm during the cold winters.

Dog Model

Dog models are used in print shoots to advertise products, as cover dog models, or as spokesdogs. Because modeling does not require that the dog be trained in specific behaviors as in animal acting (page 152), it is easier for an amateur dog to get work.

Your dog needs to be confident in an environment with distractions, such as human models, noise, and equipment such as cameras and lights. He must tolerate wearing clothing or accessories, being touched or held by a model, and being 10' (3 m) away from you. The most important training your dog will need to be a model is a solid **stay** and a **focus** command to direct his gaze.

HOW TO GET STARTED

Submit professional photos of your dog to animal talent agencies. Your dog must be well socialized and able to hold a position in a busy and unfamiliar environment.

MEET RICK CARAN & JILLI DOG
DOG MODEL

"Jilli Dog knows when the camera is on her and likes to pose! We practice 'stay,' but we add the directive 'stop.' Jilli has learned to 'stop' in a certain pose. Very handy for modeling."

RICK'S TIP: "Modeling is harder than it looks! Practice in a variety of locations."

IDEAL DOGS FOR THIS ACTIVITY:

The dog model needs to be cute, fit, clean, and well groomed.

OVERVIEW

Show off your pet and bond with your dog by walking together in a local pet parade.

A boxer struts his stuff at the annual Barkus Pet Parade in St. Louis. One of the largest pet parades in the world, eight-thousand dogs and their owners parade in colorful Mardi Gras themed costumes.

Pet Parade

Every year, towns and cities everywhere hold their version of a pet parade, giving residents an opportunity to show off their dog, cat, rabbit, pig, pony, or other beloved animal.

Many dogs wear costumes, and pet parades often award winners in a variety of categories such as best dressed and dog/owner themed costumes. A kids pets parade is common, where your children can walk or carry their animal in the parade.

HOW TO GET STARTED

Your dog should be well socialized and under your control for her first pet parade. Bring water and pick-up bags. Dogs can burn their paw pads walking on asphalt on a hot day, so check the street temperature with your hand.

MEET JIM CROSTHWAITE
WOOFSTOCK DOG FAIR ORGANIZER

"I started Woofstock to bring together local dogs and dog people. At the time, I thought I had invented the greatest name ever for a festival (only to find out later that there are several 'Woofstocks' worldwide). I guess lots of people besides me have a desire to dress up like hippies! Woofstock is a fund raiser for local dog rescue groups. Our parade is called the 'Grateful Dog Run/Walk'. Last year we had 6,000 people and are hoping for 10,000 this year. Peace!"

OVERVIEW

Does your dog roll over, play dead, or jump through a hoop? Show off his unique talent at a dog tricks contest.

Jack Russell terrier "Tayana" balances on a ball to win the "Stupid Dog Tricks" contest and a chance to perform her tricks on the televised "David Letterman Show".

Dog Trick Contest

Dog trick contests are often hosted at local dog fairs and occasionally on TV. It can take several months to perfect a trick, so train your dog now, so you'll have your trick polished! Some contestants show off a string of tricks while others perform one really killer trick!

Once your dog has learned several tricks, you can even get his **trick dog title** (see Resources, page 202). With four levels to achieve, this will keep you motivated to train.

HOW TO GET STARTED

Every dog has a trick in him—it is your job to figure it out. Watch your dog and take note of anything funny or incredible that he does naturally and develop that skill. Vocal dogs can learn to "speak" or bark an answer to a math problem. Bouncy dogs can learn to jump rope or jump through a hoop. And lazy dogs can learn to "play dead."

KYRA SUNDANCE & CHALCY
TRICK CONTEST CHAMPIONS

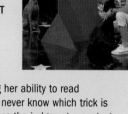

"Chalcy won the *Pet Star* TV show by demonstrating her ability to read numbers. You never know which trick is going to impress the judges at a contest, and the most difficult trick is not always the trick that wins. Sometimes a dog does a trick that is unique and funny and wins over the crowd."

KYRA'S TIP: "Every dog has a trick in them. Watch what your dog does naturally and turn that into a trick."

1 Kneel down, facing your dog. Hold several treats in your hand in front of her nose.

2 Move the treat to the side of her head opposite the direction you wish her to roll.

3 Continue to move the treat toward her shoulder blade. This should lure her to flop onto her side. Release the treat when she does.

4 Continue the motion with your hand as you move the treat from her shoulder blade toward her backbone.

5 This should lure her to roll onto her back and over to her other side.

6 Reward her the moment she lands on her opposite side.

Jack Russell Terrier "Action Jackson" performs his favorite trick—a pawstand. Jackson was adopted from the shelter on the day he was scheduled to be euthanized.

Stunt Dog Show

Entertain audiences with your own canine show! Professional stunt dog teams travel the world and are paid to perform at **fairs**, professional sporting event **halftime shows**, **circuses**, **corporate events**, **theme parks**, and **schools**. Animal entertainers are federally licensed under laws that protect the welfare of their animals and ensure that they are humanely treated and not overworked.

Shows are typically 30 minutes and are performed three times per day. School shows may incorporate more educational content and run longer, and halftime shows and circus shows last only a few minutes. Professional stunt dog teams vary widely in the number of entertainers and dogs, the amount of props, and the type of show. Some shows are athletic, featuring disc dogs, agility, flyball, and high jumping stunts. Others are more tricks oriented, incorporating comic antics, such as a dog playing basketball or playing the piano.

Although dogs are the stars of the show, the human is an entertainer as well. The audience is watching not only the dog tricks but also the interaction between the dog and the trainer. The human is an ambassador to the dog training profession, and it is his responsibility to portray a positive working relationship with his dogs.

GEAR

To entertain for a large audience, you'll need a sound system and wireless microphone (a headset microphone is convenient), crowd control gates or flags, signage, props, and costumes for yourself and your dogs. When performing on a slick surface, such as at a basketball halftime show, your dogs will need rubber booties.

HOW TO GET STARTED

Even if your dog performs perfectly in your backyard, it can be quite a different thing for him to perform in front of an audience with distractions of people, noises, smells, and food. Work the kinks out of your show in a low-stakes setting, such as a child's birthday party, a retirement home, or a church event. Your audience will be appreciative of your show even if it doesn't go exactly as planned.

Volunteer at an animal shelter **fundraising** event and teach your dog to collect donations from the audience and drop the money into a bucket.

MEET CHRIS PERONDI & JACKSON
'EXTREME CANINES' STUNT DOG SHOW

"I'm a big proponent of dog rescue, and I love showing audiences how incredible shelter dogs can be. I look in the shelters for hyper dogs that have a strong prey drive and want an active and fun lifestyle. I turn their prey drive into play drive with lots of disc, ball, and tug games.

"I never force my dogs to do a stunt that they don't enjoy. I work with each dog's natural abilities and give them roles in my show that they truly enjoy. My dogs catch discs, jump rope, do back flips, high jump, weave pole race, and do lots of amazing tricks."

CHRIS' TIP: "You need a strong bond with your dog to keep him focused on you with the distractions of a live show. During a show, you should be more fun for your dog than any of the sounds or smells around him."

IDEAL DOGS FOR THIS ACTIVITY:

Stunt show dogs should have high energy and motivation to perform several shows a day, many days in a row. Herding breeds such as border collies, Australian cattle dogs, and McNabs are common, as are Parson Russell terriers. Some acts use one specific breed, such as a poodle show or the Weimaraners used in the Sundance Dog Team.

A favorite event at fairs, dog and owner teams are judged on their resemblance to each another.

A standard poodle's fancy show cut matches her owner's interesting 'do.

Look-Alike Contest

Dog/owner look-alike contests have a long-standing tradition and are always a crowd favorite at fairs and dog events. Look-alike contests are subjectively judged, often being decided by audience applause. Rules vary but are generally very few. In some cases props and costumes are limited, and occasionally divisions separate small dogs from large dogs or purebreds from mixed breeds.

HOW TO GET STARTED

There is only so much you can do to your and your dog's physical appearance to accentuate your similarity. You can, however, dress alike and teach some behaviors that will increase your resemblance. Performing a trick in unison, such as waving at the crowd together, will make you seem more alike and will probably earn you extra votes.

IDEAL DOGS FOR THIS ACTIVITY:

Dogs in look-alike contests generally fall into one of two categories: dogs with hairstyles that resemble their owner's hairstyles and shorthaired dogs with facial features that resemble their owner's facial features.

Popular hairstyle dogs are poodles or bichon frises (which match the owner's bouffant, topknot, or ponytail style), komondors (dreadlocks), and Afghan hounds or Irish setters (with long, wavy, silky hair).

Bulldogs, bloodhounds, and greyhounds have distinctive facial features that can resemble certain people.

OVERVIEW

In this fun contest, dogs are subjectively judged on their physical appearance (shhh. . . they think it's a beauty contest!).

Two-year-old Chinese crested/Chihuahua mix "Elwood" gets prettied up with a sparkly rhinestone collar. Lovely.

Ugly Dog Contest

Ugly dogs need activities to do, too! Every year, mostly for fun, people enter their dogs into "ugly dog" contests. Despite the derogatory title, these contests really celebrate the love for dogs who are often rescued or disadvantaged. Judging is largely subjective. Veterinary screening is common to make sure the dogs are healthy. "Mutt" and pedigreed classes are sometimes separated during preliminary rounds. And that's about it for rules.

HOW TO GET STARTED

Here are a few pointers to show your dog at his best (or his worst?). Your ugly dog should look bathed and cared for, so the judges know he is loved. Hair gel can give him that "mad scientist" look, and a too-tight T-shirt will emphasize a pudgy belly. A gaudy shirt or pretty bow can add a touch of whimsy to his look.

MEET KAREN QUIGLEY & ELWOOD
WORLD'S UGLIEST DOG WINNERS

"Elwood is a rescue dog. Even though his initial appearance is odd, his loving personality shines through. I think he's the cutest thing ever!"

IDEAL DOGS FOR THIS ACTIVITY:

Mohawks, bug eyes, underbites, hairlessness, missing legs, and tongues that hang out due to a loss of teeth are winning characteristics in this contest.

Standard poodle "Cindy" is groomed as a large garden snail at the Super Groom Expo in Las Vegas, Nevada.

Creative Grooming

For creative people, creative grooming offers an artistic challenge that you can do with your dog. Creative grooming began with unusual haircuts and progressed into colored dyes, glue, feathers, and a variety of other accessories. Some dogs are groomed to look like an animal, such as a zebra, lion, or panda bear. Others have a three dimensional mural depicted across their body, such as a scenic landscape with a swooping eagle. And still others may have an intricate and brilliant pattern meticulously shaved and colored into their hair.

Creative grooming competitions are always audience favorites at shows at grooming shows and expos. Groomers have two and a half hours at a show to create their look and may present their dog with accompanying set displays, props, or costumes for themselves. Creations are judged on originality and creativity, intricacy, brilliance of coloring, decorations, and presentation. After competition, the dogs are shaved down and their groomers wait six months for their hair to grow back completely. Because of the time needed to regrow their hair, dogs can only do two contests per year.

GEAR

So how are these outrageous, over-the-top designs produced? The dogs are colored with techniques that will either wash right out, be in for a few days, or that are semi-permanent. Products include vegetable-based dyes, temporary spray hair color, blow pens that children use for watercolor art, food coloring, and colored chalk. All of the products are pet-friendly and safe. Other essentials include child-safe glue, hairspray, feathers, and rhinestones.

HOW TO GET STARTED

Creative grooming isn't just for competition, it's also a fun way to show off your dog and your personality. Spruce up your dog for special occasions by coloring his tail, ears, or topknot by applying powered colored drink mix mixed with a little water.

Try some quick-drying dog nail polish or colored rubber glue-on nail tips. There are many grooming products available, and it's safest to stick with products that are specially formulated for animals.

MEET SANDY HARTNESS & CINDY AWARD-WINNING CREATIVE GROOMER

"Cindy loves the attention she gets at creative grooming contests. I've created Cindy into a garden snail [photo, left], a camel, a peacock, a rooster, pac-man, a ninja turtle, a dragon, an alien, and many other things.

"Creative grooming combines my love for dogs and my passion for art. I get my ideas from life. An idea will just hit me and I'll grab my sketchbook and start drawing. Once I have my idea on paper, I just look at my dog and do what feels best. People think I'm crazy because I'll just grab the scissors and start whacking away; I'll just go at it. I don't do a lot of planning. The most important quality a groomer can possess is the ability to improvise."

SANDY'S TIP: "Anything safe for humans is safe for your dog and the other way around, if you would not use it on yourself, DON'T use it on your dog."

IDEAL DOGS FOR THIS ACTIVITY:

Any dog with hair long enough to style can be used for creative grooming, but white standard poodles are the breed of choice for competition.

OVERVIEW

Doga combines massage and meditation with gentle stretching for dogs and their owners.

Emily and her American Staffordshire terrier dogi "Trouble" do a 'pit-to-paw standing twist' pose. Trouble is a top-ranking show dog, and Emily is her favorite handler.

Doga

Do dogs need yoga? No, but you need yoga, and your dog needs your attention. **Doga** (yoga with your dog) offers a way to include your dog in your healthy lifestyle and to involve her in more of your life. Doga combines massage and meditation with gentle stretching. Because dogs are pack animals, they are a natural match for yoga's emphasis on union and connection with other beings.

Doga classes focus on poses and massage for dogs aimed at improving digestion and heart function and poses for people that emphasize stress reduction and feeling well. In **chaturanga**, **dogis** (dogs who practice yoga) sit with their front paws in the air while their human partners provide support. In an upward-paw pose (**super dog** or **sun salutation**), owners lift dogs onto their hind legs. In a **resting pose**, the person reclines, with legs slightly bent over the dog's torso, bolster-style, to relieve pressure on the spine.

GEAR

A yoga mat provides cushioning and traction. A standard sized yoga mat is 24" x 68" and ¼" thick (61 x 173 x 0.6 cm). Two mats can be place together to accommodate large dogis. It's best to not bring treats to doga class, as they will energize rather than relax your dog. Save the treats until after class.

HOW TO GET STARTED

Mudras are used in yoga and meditation to redirect the **prana** (life force) in the body. In doga we include our dogs in our mudras, directing prana to them and receiving it back.

Puppy Paw Mudra: Place your hands on top of your dog's front paws and think about joining your intentions.

Heart-to-Hound Mudra: Place one hand on your heart and one on your dogi's chest and focus on the love between you.

Inner Dog Mudra: Rest your forehead on your dog's forehead to connect the energy of your minds.

Barking Buddha Mudra: Place one hand on your dogi's head or upper back and the other on his lower back. Give and receive healing energy.

MEET BRENDA BRYAN & GUS
DOGA INSTRUCTOR, SEATTLE, WASHINGTON

"Doga strengthens the already amazing bond most people share with their dogs. As a doga instructor, I love witnessing a dog's natural healing ability blossom as they spend quality time with their people.

"The best thing about doga—for both yogi and dogi—is the exchange of love. It teaches us to be present with our dogs, while encouraging us to be more present and loving in all other aspects of our lives."

BRENDA'S TIP: "Build the association between the yoga mat and calmness. Introduce your dogi to your yoga mat at home and just sit quietly and hang out together. This is especially useful for training puppies, as they will become comfortable with your touch and learn to hang out with you quietly and confidently. Let your dog get used to hanging out on the mat while you move around and do poses. Once they are accustomed to the mat, incorporating your dog into the poses is easy."

IDEAL DOGS FOR THIS ACTIVITY:

Some dogs are naturally more mellow and others take longer to respond to the mellow vibe of the activity. Your dog may take a few sessions to settle in.

OVERVIEW

A gentle massage can give your dog comfort as well as aid his nervous system and increase his circulation.

A yellow Labrador retriever relaxes while getting a therapeutic massage.

Massage

Dog massage manipulates the dog's skin and muscle for a therapeutic purpose. Benefits include enhanced muscle tone and range of motion, reduction of joint inflammation and swelling, increase in the flow of nutrients to the muscles, aid in carrying away excessive fluids and toxins, and stimulation of circulation. Deep massage requires knowledge of a dog's anatomy and should be performed only by a trained and certified canine massage therapist or dog chiropractor.

HOW TO GET STARTED

Keep your home massage light and gentle. Have your dog lie on a soft, firm surface—a thick rug or carpeted floor is ideal. Start with several soft, slow strokes from head to tail. Scratch gently behind his ears, moving to his cheeks, under his chin, over his nose, between his eyes, and over his head. Rub each ear several times between your thumb and forefinger, working from base to tip.

Using three fingers, move slowly over his neck, shoulders, and chest in small, circular patterns, gently pinching folds of loose skin in these areas. Lightly squeeze down the length of each foreleg. Use your thumb and forefinger and give each foot a couple of soft squeezes.

In the second phase of the massage, place your thumb and index finger on each side of the spine and "walk" them toward the base of the tail, and then the outside of each thigh. Squeeze the length of the tail and move down the rear legs. If at any point, your dog resists, move to the last area or technique he enjoyed. Finish up with several soft, slow strokes from head to tail. Your dog will most likely be snoozing peacefully and you may be surprised to find your own tensions melted away as well.

MEET LINDA TELLINGTON-JONES
FOUNDER OF TELLINGTON TTOUCH MASSAGE METHOD

"Tellington TTouch helps to release tension and increase body awareness, allowing your dog to be handled without provoking typical fear responses. Apply it to assist with recovery from illness or injury or just to enhance the quality of your dog's life."

LINDA'S TIP: "TTouch is based on circular movements of your fingers and hands all over the dog's body. Make a connection on your dog's body with your thumb. Use your three middle fingers to push the skin on your dog in a quarter-sized circle. Then slide your hand to the next spot on his body and repeat."

IDEAL DOGS FOR THIS ACTIVITY:

Animal massage benefits dogs of any age. It can help young animals with their muscular and skeletal development, ease growing pains (especially with large breeds), and also reduce separation anxiety that a lot of puppies experience. Massage benefits dog athletes by assisting in injury prevention, shortening recovery time, and lessening the muscular/skeletal stress that can accompany changes in training routines.

Gently move the leg forward and upward, stretching the elbow and shoulder joints.

Use your hand above his knee to lift his leg gently upward and backward.

OVERVIEW

Give your dog the beauty spa experience by pampering her in all the right ways.

Afghan hounds like "Charlie" require a lot of grooming maintenance to keep their long silky hair in top condition. Adult Afghans are brushed three times a week.

Spa Day / Grooming

Pamper your dog with a spa day experience. Wash and brush her coat, clean her ears, and brush her teeth. Give her a **pawdicure** by trimming her nails and gently rubbing away any debris in the nail beds (it may help to first soak her paw in warm water). Go over her entire body, noticing any sores or abnormalities. Check her eyes for debris or cloudy spots and address with your veterinarian.

Give your pup a soothing **massage** (page 168). Give her the full experience by relaxing her with **aromatherapy**. Add a drop of vanilla, lavender, or anisette to her chew toy. **Rescue Remedy Pet** is a flower-based drops solution that is supposed to calm a stressed pet.

GEAR

Use shampoos, cleansers, and toothpastes made specifically for dogs, as human products may be too harsh.

MEET PAM LAURITZEN & DALLAS
CERTIFIED MASTER GROOMER

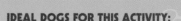

"Skin and coat care is essential to the overall health of all dogs. My Japanese Chin, Dallas, really enjoys the attention he gets during his daily grooming sessions."

IDEAL DOGS FOR THIS ACTIVITY:

Dogs vary by breed as to the amount of grooming they need, but regular grooming will help to ensure your dog is healthy and comfortable.

1 **Brush** your dog often to condition his skin and keep his coat shining.

2 **Trim your dog's nails** weekly with a scissor-like clipper or an electric dremel file.

3 **Brush your dog's teeth** every day using a toothbrush and dog toothpaste.

4 **Clean your dog's ears** every month by filling the ear with ear cleaning solution from your vet and wiping with cotton balls.

Yellow Labrador retriever "Java" accompanies wilderness guides on a hike to Crow Pass, Alaska. Java is the resident "guide dog" at the guide headquarters. Java keeps her fellow guides warm at night when camping. (She also sometimes keeps them awake, when they are visited by her nemesis.... squirrels!)

OVERVIEW

Experience the great outdoors with your dog, hiking and even spending the night together in a tent.

Hiking and Camping

Have a safe hiking and camping experience with your dog by being prepared. Dogs are much more susceptible to heat stroke than we are, so be careful to not overexert your dog. Surface water (including the purest looking of fast-flowing streams) is likely to harbor Giardia which causes diarrhea. A good rule of thumb is to carry 8 ounces (227 g) of water for your dog for every hour of planned hiking.

In addition to her normal vaccinations, consider a snake bite vaccination for your dog. When you return from a hike, check your dog's ears, nose, and eyes for abrasions and foreign bodies. Check her paws, feeling the webbing between each toe. Check her entire body for ticks and bugs, especially where her legs meet his torso and by her neck and ears.

GEAR

Have your dog carry her gear or her water with a backpack or hydration pack. Protect your dog's paws from rough or hot terrain with dog boots. Be aware that dogs dissipate heat through their tongues and paws, so boots will interfere with your dog's ability to cool herself. Used in winter, dog booties provide warmth and keep ice balls from forming between toe pads when hiking through snow. As an extra precaution, a GPS collar will help you locate your dog should she run off. In the evening, a small flashing beacon light on your dog's collar will help you keep an eye on her. A first aid kit is a good idea. If your dog ingests something potentially harmful, a few gulps of peroxide will cause her to vomit. A blaze orange collar or vest can help distinguish a dog from game during hunting season. Your dog may need a coat in cold weather and a water-soaked evaporative cool coat in hot weather.

HOW TO GET STARTED

Visit some of the many dog-friendly parks and hiking trails and be sure to check their rules ahead of time.

If you love dogs, hiking, and are interested in meeting like-minded people, consider a **hound hike**. These public programs exist at various parks and are scheduled hikes for people and their socialized, leashed dogs. Become more involved by volunteering as a hound hike leader.

MEET RICH REID & JAVA WILDERNESS GUIDES, ANCHORAGE, ALASKA

"In this photo [left], Java has her doggy panniers packed with her overnight essentials. It was the beginning of July, but there were still some snow fields on the tundra. Java loves the snow and started rolling around in it. Unfortunately she had not considered her packs and got stuck upside down like a turtle! (She didn't think it was funny)."

RICH'S TIP: "Before you hike the backcountry with your dog, familiarize him with his packs by using it on short hikes. Have your dog carry nonessential things like his own bedding or bowls (just in case he charges into the bushes after a squirrel and returns without his pack!). Know the wildlife that live in the area and be aware. Human noises will ward off most potential predators. Happy Trails."

IDEAL DOGS FOR THIS ACTIVITY:

Your dog should be obedient enough that she won't run off and can be called off of a chase. Small dogs can be in danger from predatory animals.

Bond with your dog as you experience the world together from new heights while tandem paragliding.

Yellow Labrador retriever "Hausi" paraglides over Lima, Peru. Hausi and his owner have logged over 1,000 flights together and appeared on paragliding magazine covers.

Flying Dog

If your dog loves sticking his head out the car window, wagging his tail as his ears flap in the breeze and his nose sniffs the air, then he might enjoy paragliding. **Paragliding** is flying a free-flying, foot-launched gliding parachute. The glider pilot is suspended below a fabric wing by sitting in a harness in a "lounge chair" position. He launches by running (or skiing) down a slope into the wind.

Paragliding pilots around the world have endeavored to share their sport with their dogs by constructing attachments that allow their dog to ride tandem. The dog can be positioned to the front or side of the pilot, but most pilots position their dog in their lap, relieving the pressure of his harness. During turns, the dog may try to shift to keep himself vertical.

GEAR

The dog wears a super-secure harness that gives him comfortable support. Search-and-rescue dogs are sometimes lowered by a harness from a helicopter. These secure harnesses can be purchased and are found in categories such as SAR harnesses or K-9 rappel harnesses. They can be attached to your rig via several carabiner clips.

HOW TO GET STARTED

You should be a licensed and experienced paraglider before bringing your dog. Help your dog develop a positive association with his harness by putting it on him at home and giving him praise and treats. Use a harness hanging rig to adjust your harnesses to a position that is comfortable for your dog. Swing with your dog gently to simulate the swing of a paraglider.

Your dog's first flight should be a short, two-minute flight at a training hill. Be aware that you landing may be a little faster than normal, due to the extra weight.

MEET JOSÉ ROSAS & HAUSI
LIMA, PERU

"Hausi is named after Hausi Bolinger, a world champion paraglider. When Hausi was just a month old I wrapped him in a sock and attached him at my chest and took him on his first flight. Hausi has since done over a thousand flights with me and even made a flying dog-girlfriend in Alaska (her name is Leah).

"I own a paragliding school, and every day Hausi insists on getting the first ride. He brings his harness to me to let me know that he is ready to go. His favorite part is the launch—he gets so excited and runs toward the cliff. When we are flying he likes to look around. He lives free on the beach where we live and spends his days playing at the shore."

JOSÉ'S TIP: "Paragliding is an incredible sport, but it must be learned from professionals. Look for a good paragliding school and ask to do a tandem flight with the instructor."

IDEAL DOGS FOR THIS ACTIVITY:

Short-nosed (*brachycephalic*) dogs often have problems with breathing and overheating when they are nervous and therefore should never be taken flying.

OVERVIEW

Let your dog run off leash and socialize with others of his species at a dog park.

DOGS AT PLAY

Some dog parks feature beautiful nat ral settings and even a water area for your dog to swim in!

Off-Leash Dog Park

A dog park is a facility set aside for dogs to exercise and play off leash in a controlled environment under the supervision of their owners. Dog parks may also feature agility equipment, a pond for swimming, and a separate enclosure for small dogs.

Basic good manners are a park prerequisite. Your dog should not body-slam, mouth, jump on kids, or mark (leg-lift) humans in the park, nor should he jump into laps of random sitting humans without invitation.

HOW TO GET STARTED

Remove your dog's leash as soon as you enter the off-leash area. Mixing on-leash and off-leash dogs can cause stress in the leashed dogs, which may lead to aggression. Limit your use of toys or food treats to avoid conflict between dogs.

MEET CESAR MILAN STAR OF "THE DOG WHISPERER"

Cesar recommends not using the dog park as a substitute for a walk! If you drive to the park, leave your car a block away and take your dog on a vigorous walk of at least 35 minutes to drain some of her energy before entering the park. Never take an overexcited dog to the park.

IDEAL DOGS FOR THIS ACTIVITY:

Dogs with serious behavior problems with other dogs or humans should not visit a dog park.

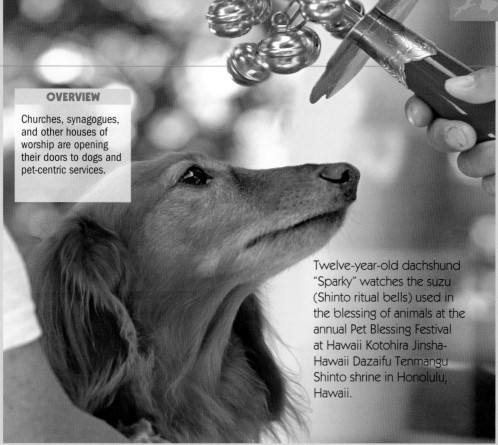

OVERVIEW

Churches, synagogues, and other houses of worship are opening their doors to dogs and pet-centric services.

Twelve-year-old dachshund "Sparky" watches the suzu (Shinto ritual bells) used in the blessing of animals at the annual Pet Blessing Festival at Hawaii Kotohira Jinsha-Hawaii Dazaifu Tenmangu Shinto shrine in Honolulu, Hawaii.

Canines at Prayer

A growing number of congregations are holding regular pet blessings and pet-centric services as a way to build their congregations. Many churches have opened their doors once a week to allow canines at covenant, with the intention of addressing the spirituality of pets and the deeply felt bonds that owners form with their animals. This has reinvigorated the church's community outreach and attracted new members.

During the 30-minute worship, dogs sit on the pews or under the pews on comfortable rugs. Once service begins, most of the yipping subsides, and the dogs lay calmly (for the most part!). There are canine prayers and a tray of dog treats for the offering.

Many houses of worship sponsor an annual **blessing of the animals** in October, in honor of the feast day for St. Francis of Assisi.

MEET BETTY YAMASAKI & JACKIE

"About 400 dogs participate in the Pet Blessing Festival at Hawaii Kotohira Jinsha-Hawaii Dazaifu Tenmangu. It is a special day and blessing for these and all animals to be respected and appreciated for their unconditional love and friendship that they show. Our pets are spiritual creatures that nurture us unconditionally. It creates a day of love and celebration honoring our faithful friends and loyal companions."

IDEAL DOGS FOR THIS ACTIVITY:

Well-trained dogs and mellow dogs are ideal for the stillness of a church.

Certified therapy dogs cheer people up by visiting them in hospitals or other facilities.

Eight-year-old Newfoundland therapy dog "Gus" comforts a patient at a children's hospital. Gus has been specially trained to visit with children.

THERAPY DOG

Therapy Dog

"Why do you come here?" asked a patient as he petted a therapy dog.

"How do you feel when you pet my dog?" The dog's owner asked. The patient smiled, "I feel good."

"That's why I come."

Volunteering as a **certified therapy dog team** is a rewarding way to share your dog and bring smiles to the faces of people you visit. Therapy dogs offer unconditional love and warmth to people in difficult times, providing comfort and a friendly distraction from stress or pain.

A therapy dog's primary job is to allow unfamiliar people to pet or hug him and to enjoy that contact. The dog might need to be lifted onto or climb onto a patient's lap or bed and sit or lie there comfortably. Some dogs contribute to the visiting experience by performing simple tricks.

Many hospitals are proud to have therapy dogs visit their facility and recognize the health benefits these visits can provide. Hospitals' volunteer departments usually coordinate these planned visits with local therapy dog groups. In addition to **hospitals**, therapy dogs also visit **assisted living** or **nursing care facilities**, **hospices**, **schools**, and **shelters** and can also aid in **disaster stress relief**.

GEAR

Once certified, therapy dog teams wear a uniform on their visits, often an imprinted shirt for the handler and an identifying **cape** for the dog.

HOW TO GET STARTED

Therapy dogs become certified through a series of tests by a certified evaluator. Tests include a temperament evaluation, which sometimes includes the **Canine Good Citizen** test (see page 124). The dog is also tested on his reaction to unusual sounds and behavior, such as a person using a wheelchair, crutches, or other service equipment or moving or speaking erratically.

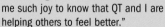

MEET CAROLE KELLY & QT
THERAPY DOG TESTER/OBSERVER

"I've been involved with dog therapy for 25 years now, and it brings me such joy to know that QT and I are helping others to feel better."

CAROLE'S TIP: "Socialize your dog by taking him with you to all sorts of places. Don't pressure him to approach fearful things, but give him time to investigate them on his own. Ask people if they want to pet your dog."

IDEAL DOGS FOR THIS ACTIVITY:

Therapy dogs come in all sizes and breeds. The most important characteristic of a therapy dog is his temperament: he must be friendly, patient, confident, gentle, and at ease in all situations. Therapy dogs must enjoy human contact and be content to be petted and handled, sometimes clumsily.

Not all dogs are suited to every environment. Some interact better with children, while others are better suited with adults. Different dogs respond with more or less ease to erratic or excited human behavior. Therapy dogs must be at least one year old.

Children improve their literacy skills by reading aloud to a dog (which is less intimidating than reading to a parent or teacher).

Trained therapy dog Irish setter "Ross" listens to a student read. Each week students who struggle with reading get a private 30-minute session with Ross or another therapy dog.

Literacy Dogs

Children who have difficulty reading can be reluctant to read aloud for fear of having their mistakes criticized or laughed at. But a dog will never laugh at them and will always be an appreciative audience. A child's literacy skills can be improved through the assistance of registered therapy dogs and their handlers as literacy mentors.

Volunteer teams go to schools and libraries as reading companions for children. One child will read to a dog for about 15–30 minutes, while the dog's handler listens as well. Children enjoy being the teacher, or storyteller, to the dog and will even hold up the book for the dog to see the pictures or ask the dog which book he would like to hear next.

The human volunteer speaks for the dog, thereby encouraging the child to make a connection with the dog. If the child doesn't know a word in her book, for example, the human volunteer says that the dog doesn't know the word either. This makes the child feel that she is not alone. The child and the dog can then look up the word in the dictionary together.

HOW TO GET STARTED

Literacy dog programs exist around the world, such as **Reading Education Assistance Dogs** (R.E.A.D.) in the United States, Canada, United Kingdom, and beyond. Most teams are required to be certified therapy dog teams (see page 178).

Canine Ambassador

Another way to help children is by becoming an ambassador for responsible dog ownership by making presentations in classrooms, libraries, after-school programs, and youth group meetings such as Boy/Girl Scouts and 4-H. Volunteer programs exist within national kennel clubs to support ambassadors with presentation material.

HOW TO GET STARTED

The kennel club provides you with an information packet which includes guidelines for developing your program, reproducibles, promotional brochures to give to teachers or parents, and a lapel pin. Your name is added to a directory for teachers to contact you, or you can reach out to schools in your area.

MEET EMILY,
READER, AGE 6

"It seems like the dogs listen more. Mostly when you read to people they're looking around, not listening to you. The dog sits there and doesn't interrupt. He doesn't ask questions like people. My favorite thing I like about Toby is that he shakes hands and barks to say 'bye' to me."

MEET SANDI MARTIN
INTERMOUNTAIN THERAPY ANIMALS

"One young child arrived at the library for the first time to read to my dog. His head down and speaking in a whisper, he told me, 'I don't read very well.' The first week he only read a half a book. By the fourth week, his attitude was far different. He came running in and in a loud voice exclaimed to my dog, 'I have a really cool book to read to you today! You're going to love it!'"

IDEAL DOGS FOR THIS ACTIVITY:

Dogs should have solid obedience skills and be calm and comfortable being touched and be able to deal with unexpected encounters with rambunctious children, loud noises, and a school setting. Older dogs are often suited for this activity.

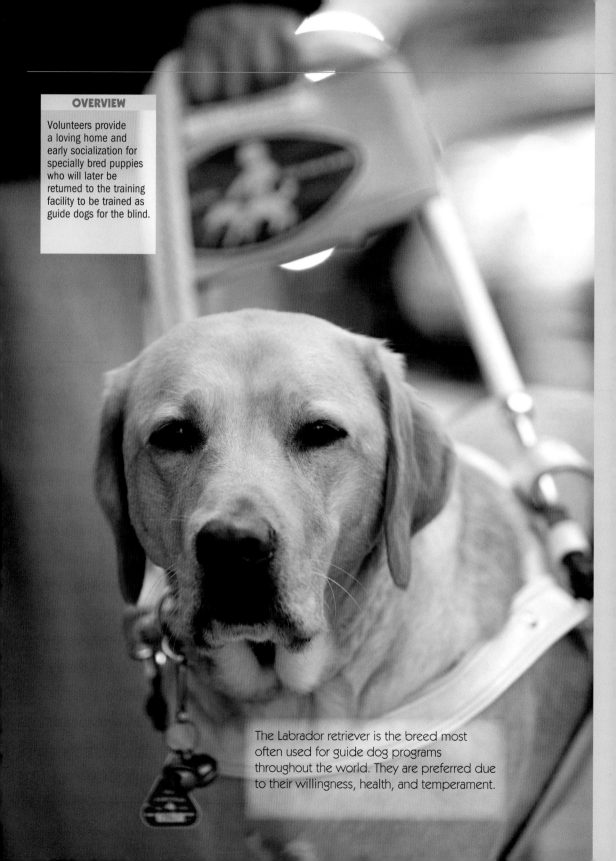

OVERVIEW

Volunteers provide a loving home and early socialization for specially bred puppies who will later be returned to the training facility to be trained as guide dogs for the blind.

The Labrador retriever is the breed most often used for guide dog programs throughout the world. They are preferred due to their willingness, health, and temperament.

Guide Dog Puppy Raiser

A guide dog is specially trained to **pilot** his blind owner by helping to navigate traffic, stairs, and sidewalks while avoiding obstacles. Guide dog training schools have their own breeding programs to produce the next generation of guide dogs. When the puppies are eight weeks old, they are placed with volunteer **puppy raisers**, who provide a loving home and early training during a puppy's first year of life in order to prepare the puppy for his formal guide dog training.

Puppy raisers provide socialization for the puppy through extensive exposure to people, animals, and public places, so that the puppies become comfortable in a wide variety of situations. Puppies accompany their raisers just about everywhere, including grocery stores, school and work, restaurants, shops, cars, and planes. Puppies wear a "Guide Dog in Training" cape in public that gains them entrance into some places where other dogs may not be allowed. Puppy raisers teach the puppy basic obedience and manners, housebreaking, waiting at doors, riding in cars, and walking on a leash.

At approximately 13 to 18 months of age, puppies are recalled to their guide dog training school for formal training. After four months of guide dog training, raisers are invited to attend their dogs' graduation ceremony and formally present the dog they raised to their new blind partners. (Dogs that do not excel in their guide dog training are **career changed** and are often adopted as pets by their puppy raisers.)

Certain dogs are selected as breeding stock dogs, who will produce the next litter of prospective guide dog puppies. These dogs are placed in the homes of volunteer **breeding stock custodians**, who provide day-to-day care. Custodians bring the dog to the breeding facility as required (brood bitches may require eight to ten round trips per year since they are required to be boarded in a kennel when they are in season; stud dogs may require as many as fifteen trips).

HOW TO GET STARTED

No prior experience is necessary to become a puppy raiser, and you will receive expert local guidance through a puppy raising club. It is a rewarding, emotional experience. Puppy raisers are also needed for other types of service dogs, such as **Canine Companions for Independence** and other international organizations (see Resources, page 202).

MEET NANNETTE KLATT & FLAME
BLIND ACTRESS, AND GUIDE DOG

"I'm grateful to have had four guide dog partners (all Dobermans). Every day when I take hold of the harness, I entrust my safety to my guide dog. She has never failed me.

"The most influential time in a guide dog's life begins with the puppy raiser who takes the puppy into her arms, her heart, and her home. A puppy raiser is not a nine-to-five job—it is twenty-four–seven and takes true conviction, compassion and courage. When a puppy raiser's job is done, her heart will break and tears will fall. But the greatest joy of all will come when the puppy she once held so dear and so tightly in her arms becomes the eyes for someone else. One journey comes to an end for the puppy, and another journey begins. Behind every great guide dog is a great puppy raiser. I am sincerely grateful for the selfless work you do. Thank you."

IDEAL DOGS FOR THIS ACTIVITY:

The most common guide dog breed is the Labrador retriever (due to their intelligence, work ethic, and early maturation). Also common are the golden retriever, German shepherd dog, golden/Lab cross (goldador), and Lab/poodle cross (labradoodle), as well as poodle, collie, vizsla, Doberman, Rottweiler, boxer, and Airedale terrier.

Specially trained service dogs assist a people with disabilities.

Yellow Labrador retriever service dog "Endal" helps his owner open a train door. Endal has been awarded the Gold Medal for Animal Gallantry and Devotion to Duty, the highest award available to an animal.

Service Dog

A service dog (also called an **assistance dog**) is specially trained to help a person with a particular disability. There are different types of service dogs. **Guide dogs** guide their blind owners around obstacles and through traffic. **Hearing dogs** alert their deaf owners to particular sounds such as a doorbell. A **mobility assist** dog may be trained to pull a wheelchair, pick things up from the floor, open and close doors, or pull a seated person to a standing position. A **seizure alert/ response** dog is trained to alert when his owner is about to have a seizure or to respond during a seizure by staying with his owner. Other service dogs can alert to hypoglycemia in their **diabetic** owner. Some dogs are trained to hit a special button that phones emergency services. A **psychiatric service dog** stabilizes his owner, for example when the owner suffers from a panic attack. A **social signal dog** is trained to alert a person with **autistic** symptoms to their repetitive movements. The dog acts as an attention-focuser, interrupting his partner's train of thought.

All service dogs learn a working position, usually the heel position, which the dog is responsible for maintaining regardless of how the owner moves and whether or not the leash is dropped. By law, disabled persons may be accompanied by their working service dogs into restaurants and buildings that may not otherwise allow dogs. When you meet a working service dog, be considerate by not petting or distracting the dog.

GEAR

Service dogs are trained to behave one way when working and allowed to just be dogs when they aren't. Typically they are taught to know work versus relaxation by whether or not they are wearing their gear. Service dogs often wear a cape which identifies them as a working service dog. The owner often carries an identification card which identifies himself and his dog as a working team.

HOW TO GET STARTED

Some service dogs are bred and trained by service dog organizations. There are many programs that can train your own dog to be a service dog and can train you to handle your service dog. One common task a service dog learns is to retrieve an object for his owner (purse, dropped pencil, medication, etc.). Teach your dog to fetch (page 96).

MEET ALLEN PARTON & ENDAL
EX-ROYAL NAVY CHIEF PETTY OFFICER AND HIS AWARD-WINNING SERVICE DOG

Endal learned to respond to hundreds of instructions and signed commands. He could retrieve items from supermarket shelves, operate buttons and switches, and load and empty a washing machine. He was able to put a card into an automated teller machine, punch in Allen's PIN code, retrieve the card when the process was complete, and return the card to a wallet.

Once, Allen was knocked out of his wheelchair by a speeding car and left unconscious in a car park. Endal pulled Allen into the recovery position, covered him with a blanket, and fetched his mobile phone from under the car. Getting no response, Endal then left Allen's side and went to a nearby hotel and raised the alarm.

Allen and Endal's story became a bestselling book entitled *Endal* and is being made into a feature movie.

ALLEN SAYS: "Endal never judges me or turns away because of my condition. His love is unconditional and he is helping me become more tolerant in life. Every day we learn another way in which we can work together as a team. There seems to be no limits to what we can achieve together!"

IDEAL DOGS FOR THIS ACTIVITY:

Any breed of dog can be a service dog. The dog must be able to focus and have a good work ethic. Service dogs should be well socialized and comfortable in a variety of public settings. They should have a good temperament, good health including physical structure, biddability, and trainability.

OVERVIEW

Open your home to a dog who needs a place to live and learn until he finds his permanent home.

A volunteer takes a yellow Labrador retriever from the shelter to her home to give him some training and socialization.

Foster a Dog

Open your home to a dog who needs a place to live and learn until he can find a home. Many animal shelters struggle to provide enough space to house homeless dogs. And many homeless dogs need to be socialized before they are adoptable. Fostering a dog is a great way to help.

Volunteer foster homes are needed to care for young puppies until they are old enough for adoption, for special needs dogs who require extra care, and for sick or injured dogs undergoing veterinary treatment. Foster homes provide dogs a chance to be out of a cage and an opportunity to get used to a home environment.

HOW TO GET STARTED

You can foster a dog on a long-term basis or just take him home for the weekend. Contact your local animal shelter or rescue organization.

MEET PATTY ETHERINGTON & IZUMI
KOREAN JINDO RESCUE

"Fostering a deserving dog is one of the most rewarding experiences in my life. Many Jindos are given up because their owners are not prepared to deal with the territorial temperament of this breed. Taking in a dog who has been rejected by his owner and then showing him love and watching him blossom into the creature God meant him to be is an honor. And then of course, there are the infamous failed fosters (of which I now have three!)."

IDEAL DOGS FOR THIS ACTIVITY:

Every dog deserves a **forever home**, and any time or energy you can give to adoptable dogs is a wonderful gift.

OVERVIEW

Get fit by going for a run with a shelter dog. The dogs will love the exercise and exposure the world.

tulsaspca.org

American foxhound mix "Boomer" and akita mix "Trevor" sport yellow "adopt me" bandanas when they run with volunteer runners and walkers from the SPCA shelter. Some volun eers end up adopting a dog they run!

Jog a Shelter Dog

Animal shelters need dog lovers just like you to walk and exercise dogs and provide them with human companionship. Vigorous exercise benefits dogs that are confined to kennels, and regular outings improve them emotionally and socially, making them more likely to be adopted.

Exercise programs enlist local volunteer runners and walkers to take the dogs out on roads or trails. The dogs love the attention and the sense of freedom and adventure, and the runner may enjoy companionship and even protection. Dogs wear vests or bandanas advertising that they are adoptable, and runners act as ambassadors to the shelter, stopping to answer questions about the dog.

HOW TO GET STARTED

Volunteers must be in reasonably good physical condition, have dog handling experience, and attend an orientation meeting at the shelter.

MEET ALAN WARD & KELBY
FOUNDER, 'GET FIT WITH FIDO'

"I enjoy running with a dog, but I couldn't keep a dog where I was living, so I took shelter dogs on my runs. My favorite running partner was a special German shepherd/kuvasz mix named Kelby. Due to Kelby, I started running more consistently (because I couldn't miss an appointment with him!).

"Kelby was adopted Christmas Eve. When I went to the shelter to say goodbye, I was told he had just left with his new family. I was given a Christmas ornament with Kelby's picture on it, and I still have that 'badge of honor.' It means more to me than all my trophies and ribbons from my competitive running days."

OVERVIEW

Serve your community while you walk your dog by educating and helping park visitors.

"Brownie" is one of many dogs who patrol park trails and help visitors share the trails responsibly. Below, chocolate Labrador retriever "Coco" and German shepherd dog "Bodie" take their recertification test.

Volunteer Dog Patrol

Volunteer dog patrol teams are human/dog teams who act as a specialized safety patrol team for a parks department. They assist the park ranger department by walking and hiking park trails with their dog, acting as **goodwill ambassadors** for the park district, and by **observing**, **reporting**, and **educating** park users. They help park visitors find their way around, stay safe, and follow the rules.

Though dog patrol members have the same responsibilities as do the members of other safety patrol teams, their special interest is to meet other park visitors who walk with dogs, to provide them with education and safety advice, and to encourage them to follow rules about dogs in our parklands. They help to protect the safety of visitors and their dogs, protect and preserve park plants, wildlife, and trail, and promote enjoyable experiences for visitors.

Both the dog and handler must be trained and certified and are often required to patrol a minimum number of hours per week and attend membership meetings.

Teams also assist at park-sponsored special events and festivals and represent the park in area parades.

GEAR

Volunteer dog patrol members carry ID cards. Teams wear green imprinted uniform shirts and dog capes and sometimes carry a radio to communicate with dispatch.

HOW TO GET STARTED

Your dog must be well-trained and be sociable with people and with other dogs. To allow these characteristics to be evaluated, you and your dog are given a certification test similar to the Canine Good Citizen test (page 124). If there is no volunteer dog patrol group in your area, consider working with your parks department to develop one. Similar to Neighborhood Watch groups, dog walker patrols can be organized to keep watch on your neighborhood.

MEET HEATHER GILFILLAN & LUCY
COMPANION DOG PATROL COORDINATOR

"My daughter picked my dog Lucy out from the shelter. She is part basenji and part dachshund, super smart, and loves to learn tricks. She doesn't do Companion Dog Patrol though because I think she has the dog equivalent of ADD and OCD.

"Our Dog Patrol has 15 volunteers who patrol over 100,000 acres of parkland. The program grew out of our Hiking Patrol program, which had some members who wanted to enjoy the outdoors with their canine companions. Dog patrollers not only get to enjoy the beautiful parks, but they also get to enjoy them with their canine companions."

HEATHER'S TIP: "There is a fair amount of walking and hiking in this activity, so you and your dog should physically conditioned."

IDEAL DOGS FOR THIS ACTIVITY:

Dogs should be calm, friendly, and not easily spooked. They need to be under voice control.

Handicapped dogs "Pitzi" (left) and "Doll" walk with their wheelchairs during a pets' rights parade in Lima, Peru. The parade was organized to promote orphaned pets' adoption and rights.

Physically Challenged Dogs

With the assistance of mobility devices, a physically challenged dog can lead a happy and active life. A **dog wheelchair** can enable your dog to run, play, and exercise again. Wheelchairs are used for dogs with hip and leg problems or leg amputations. Dogs who have trouble standing up, walking, and supporting their rear end can be assisted with a **support harness or sling**. The harness wraps around your dog's hips or chest and has a handle on the top which you use to lift him to his feet or to partially support his weight as he walks.

Pet steps are a set of two or three stairs that your dog can use to more easily walk up onto furniture or a bed. Handy collapsible **pet ramps** assist your dog into and out of your car and are recommend for pets with orthopedic problems, osteo arthritis, hip dysplasia, and shoulder, leg, or back problems.

Hydrotherapy (page 76) is a great way for your physically challenged dog to exercise and stretch his muscles and joints.

MEET BRANDON WARING & SKY
DOG-WHEELCHAIR MAKER

"Our American Staffordshire terrier, Sky, was born blind. I taught her all kinds of tricks like 'shell game,' 'find the hidden veggies,' and 'which hand holds the treat' (Sky likes to use her nose!).

"Even though Sky can't get around like other dogs, she still craves attention and mental stimulation just like every other dog. Disabled dogs don't need pity—they need rich, full, rewarding lives. Blind, deaf, and crippled dogs rule!"

OVERVIEW

Your dog can help save dogs' lives by donating much needed blood.

Six-year-old Rottweiler "Cody" is a regular blood donor, visiting the donation center every six months.

Blood Donor Dog

Every day, dogs just like yours need blood transfusions. Without dog blood donors, veterinary surgeons could not undertake important and often life-saving operations. Blood donor dogs undergo a half-hour session and are sometimes compensated with a gift basket. Dogs are also promised blood if they ever need transfusions themselves.

HOW TO GET STARTED

Donor dogs must be friendly, obedient, and even-tempered. Because of the costs involved in the health screening and blood testing, blood donation centers are looking for people who are willing to bring their dogs to donate blood regularly, about two to three times per year. Make the blood donation center a happy place by taking your dog to the center on days when they aren't donating, to just say "hi."

MEET GENNIPHER STEMPLEWSKI & SHADOW

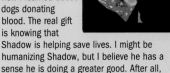

"I donate blood myself, which is how I learned about dogs donating blood. The real gift is knowing that Shadow is helping save lives. I might be humanizing Shadow, but I believe he has a sense he is doing a greater good. After all, Great Danes are working dogs!"

IDEAL DOGS FOR THIS ACTIVITY:

A dog must be between 1 and 7 years of age, and over 50 pounds (23 kg). There are over a dozen blood types in dogs, but only dogs with a universal blood type are used as donors. About 40 percent of all dogs have a universal blood type, but over 60 percent of greyhounds have it.

Chihuahua "Zee" adds his painted pawprints to a canvas filled with prints from dogs available for adoption as part of an animal care center fund raiser.

Pawprint Painting

Have fun with your dog while creating lasting memories and creative artwork through pawprint painting. The simplest painting method is **partner pawprint painting** (see photo, left.) Lay poster paper (white or colored) on the ground on a hard surface. Pour several colors of children's paint onto paper plates and gently press your dog's paws into the paint. Guide him to walk on the paper for an impressionist-style work of art!

In **target paw painting**, your dog learns to **target** (touch with his paw) a plate of paint and then target the canvas. (See instructions on teaching your dog to touch a target on page 154). The dog can wear a bootie to soak up the paint and produce nice streaks. For a softer look, try water color paints.

A master artist can learn to hold a T-shaped paintbrush in his mouth and do **paintbrush art**. Dip the paintbrush into paint and train your dog to grab it by the handle and touch the canvas with the brush.

Add your own creative touch to your dog's artwork by making **paw posies**. Press your dog's pawprint onto the canvas and then finish the painting by turning his pawprints into colorful flowers.

Use scratch art paper to create **scratch art**. The paper initially appears black, but where your dog scratches it, brilliant color is revealed below.

Mat and frame your picture and hang it on the wall, or design pawprint note cards, or even try a paint your own pottery store. Don't forget to have your pooch **pawtograph** the bottom corner of his masterpieces by placing a clear pawprint as his signature.

GEAR

Use children's paint (which is nontoxic and washable) or a rich mixture of colored powdered drink mix.

HOW TO GET STARTED

See examples of the different types of paw paintings on the following pages. Be sure to have your clean-up strategy prepared before you dip into the paint (such as a bucket or childrens' wading pool prefilled with water).

MEET PATSY HELMETAG & EDDIE
PAW POSIES CREATOR

"I was painting in my studio one day when my Labrador Eddie accidently stepped in an open palette of yellow paint on the floor and then walked across some paper. Rather than getting upset, my partner put some flourishes on the paw prints and voila—art!

"Eddie's yellow paw prints turned into a business, and we now sell kits that allow people to have their own dog prints turned into floral art. Every dog can be a Pawcasso!"

PATSY'S TIP: "Every paw print has unique characteristics. We want to keep the integrity of the paw print, and so we avoid painting in these spots."

IDEAL DOGS FOR THIS ACTIVITY:

Some dogs naturally paw or scratch at things more than other dogs, so this may influence which type of pawpainting you try. Most dogs have a paw preference; they are either right or left-handed. Encourage your dog to paint with his dominant paw.

Scratch Art: Ten-year-old Jack Russell terrier Tillamook Cheddar, or Tillie, has been painting since she was a puppy and collaborated with major established artists. Tillie's paintings sell for a handsome price in art shows and galleries.

Target Paw Painting: Blue tick beagle "Bear" ("Baron von Beaglestein") loves paw painting. He is very deliberate in where the paint goes! No matter how his owner moved the board from side to side in this photo, he only painted that one corner. When he was finished and his owner turned it over, she found he had painted a camp fire! Notice Bear's pawtograph in the corner.

Paw Posies: Turn your dog's paw prints into floral paw posy art. Each set of paw prints is as different as each dog and will inspire a different flower.

Paintbrush Art: Sammy, a foxhound mix, uses a paintbrush attached to a rubber bone, to paint his canvas. Some of Sammy's paintings are all the rage with hip New York galleries.

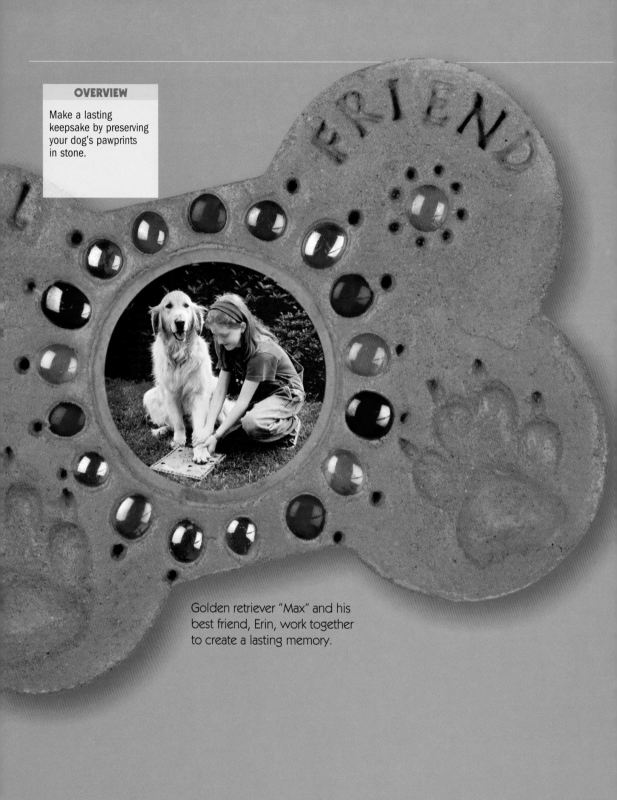

OVERVIEW

Make a lasting keepsake by preserving your dog's pawprints in stone.

Golden retriever "Max" and his best friend, Erin, work together to create a lasting memory.

Pawprint Memory Stone

A **pawprint memory stone** is a great way to personalize your garden, give as a gift, or preserve as a keepsake.

YOU WILL NEED

Gather the following: a mold (such as a clear plastic planter saucer, a pie tin, or a square mold made by nailing a wooden framework); quick-drying cement or concrete; embellishments to decorate your stone; and petroleum jelly.

DIRECTIONS

1. Mix the concrete and fill the mold half full. Gently tap around the outside of the mold to help remove any air bubbles and to smooth out the top.

2. Leave your stepping stone for 30 to 60 minutes until it has started to set.

3. Coat your dog's paw with petroleum jelly, making sure to coat between each of his toes.

4. Now it's time for your dog to put his paw into the mixture (this is the tricky part!). The pawprint will turn out best if your dog stands on the foot with his own weight, rather than having you press his paw into the concrete. Put your dog next to the mold. Lift his chest so both front feet come off the ground. Curl back the wrist of one paw as you lower him so that his other front paw lands in the concrete with all of his weight on the paw in the mold. Lift him off by his chest and do the other foot. If the pawprint did not come out well, smooth out the concrete and try again.

5. Add some glass beads for decoration or use bone-shaped cookie cutters to make designs. Once the concrete has fully set, remove it from the mold.

Another variation of this arts and crafts project is to take the cast paw print, rub it with petroleum jelly, and fill it with modeling clay. Carefully extract the clay and bake it per the instructions on the package. The result will be a 3D paw!

MEET ERIN BIRMINGHAM & MAX
PAW PRINT COVER MODELS

"When I was 10, my mom was working at a company that made a pawprint stepping stone kit product. They were having a photo shoot for the product packaging, and at the last minute they decided to take a photo of Max and me [photo left]. That photo is still on the package of their product today. (My mom thinks that photo is responsible for the great sales.)

"We had to put Max down when he was 13 due to his difficulty in breathing from esophageal paralysis. And I'm now a senior in college, so a lot has changed since the day we made our pawprint stone together. It's little things like that, though, that become cherished memories."

ERIN'S TIP: "It's very easy to do, really. I guess my main tip would be to wash your dog's paws well after putting them in the concrete."

IDEAL DOGS FOR THIS ACTIVITY:

A pawprint memory stone will be cherished long after the dog has left your life. Make one today—you'll be glad you did.

OVERVIEW

Spend an afternoon with your best buddy baking up some homemade doggy treats. Yum!

Golden retriever "Ronja" does quality control as her owner prepares biscuits in their 'Dog's Goodies' dog bakery in Wiesbaden, Germany. The bakery caters specially to dogs with offerings such as minty biscuits, muesli bars, tuna cakes, garlic cookies, and even birthday cakes complete with sausage toppings and candles.

Homemade Dog Treats

Sure, you can buy a variety of dog treats from the pet store, but sometimes it's more fun to bake them up yourself (with your dog as the taste tester!). In addition to providing your dog with nutritious, homemade treats, home cooking lets you nurture your dog with the same love and care that you lavish on the human members of your family.

Tie the treats with a ribbon and give them away as party favors at a dog party or as holiday gifts to your dog-loving friends.

Warning: some human foods can be toxic to your dog. Don't feed your dog chocolate, onions, macadamia nuts, avocado, alcohol, coffee, coffee beans, tea, raisins, or grapes.

PEANUT BUTTER HEARTS

Every dog loves peanut butter, and these easy-to-make **peanut butter hearts** will make him drool!

INGREDIENTS

4 cups (480 g) whole wheat flour
2 cups (230 g) wheat germ
2 cups (520 g) peanut butter
1½ cups (355 ml) water
¼ cup (85 g) honey
¼ cup (38 g) ground peanuts

DIRECTIONS

1. Place all ingredients in a large bowl. Mix thoroughly to combine.

2. Roll out dough on floured surface to about ¼" (6 mm) thick. Using a cookie cuter, cut into heart shapes. Combine dough scraps and continue to roll out and cut into shapes until all dough has been used.

3. Place cookies on ungreased foil-lined baking sheets and bake in a preheated 325°F (170°C, or gas mark 3) oven for 30 to 35 minutes. Makes 5 to 6 dozen cookies.

MEET MARK BECKLOFF
COFOUNDER, THREE DOG BAKERY

"Three Dog Bakery is the world's original bakery for dogs and now a chain known the entire world rover. My partner Dan Dye and I (along with dogs Sarah, Dottie, and Gracie) started it out of genuine lifelong love and respect for dogs and in appreciation for the joy dogs bring into the world. We wanted to bring healthful, fresh food to our furry buddies—an approach that was not available in the late 1980s.

"Our company's treats and foods are wholesome, healthy, fresh-baked (and pawsitively de-leash-ous!) and include tail-wagging favorites such as: Pupcakes, Rollovers, SnickerPoodles, and Great Danish. You can see some of our recipes on our cooking show for dogs called *Three Dog Bakery ... Unleashed!*"

IDEAL DOGS FOR THIS ACTIVITY:

Dogs with finicky taste or special dietary needs will definitely benefit from home cooking, however every dog will enjoy your special treats!

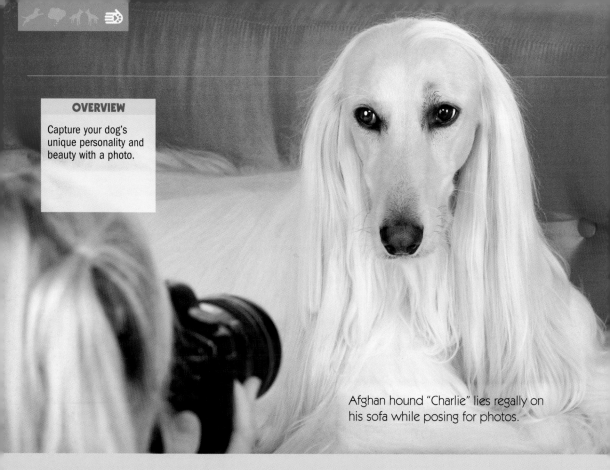

OVERVIEW

Capture your dog's unique personality and beauty with a photo.

Afghan hound "Charlie" lies regally on his sofa while posing for photos.

Phodography

Natural light is the easiest to work with, whether outdoors or near a big picture window. This will give you warm hues without harsh shadows. Get down on your dog's level and zoom in tight. Try a **wide-angle lens**, which will make your dog's head appear larger, giving him a cute puppy-dog look. To get a dog to stay put, try placing him on a chair or on top of a box.

HOW TO GET STARTED

Amateur and professional photographers shoot dogs in competition at dog shows and then offer the photos for sale on their websites. Many dog clubs will hire an official photographer to take pictures of the competition winners. You can practice your technique by volunteering to take engaging photos of adoptable animals at the animal shelter for display on their website.

MEET NICK SAGLIMBENI
PHOTOGRAPHER

NICK'S TIP:
"Use a squeak toy to get your dog to prick his ears, cock his head, and give an alert look. Dogs are very smart, though, and this trick only works a few times before they just ignore it. You have to keep trying new noises and toys."

IDEAL DOGS FOR THIS ACTIVITY:

Dogs with dark-colored faces will be harder to photograph, as they will require more precise lighting.

Make your dog's special day even more special with cake, presents, doggy friends, and doggy games!

This happy bearded collie is celebrating the anniversary of his adoption into his family. Lucky dog!

Doggy Birthday Party

Your dog is a part of your family, and you want to make his birthday a special day for him. Make your own cake and treats or purchase healthy fare from a dog bakery. Your dog may enjoy doggy guests from his daycare or play group. You can host your party at your home, at a dog park, doggy day care, pet resort, or pet store.

Plan some fun party games for the dogs such as a whipped-cream-pie eating contest, pawpainting (page 192), pawprint memory stones (page 196), or weenie bobbing (toss some hot dogs into a wading pool filled with water and let the dogs fish them out). Don't forget to take photos!

Plan some gifts for your guests to take home, such as personalized water bowls (which will be helpful during the party.) And if your dog doesn't mind, dress her up with a special birthday bandana or party dress.

MEET PATRICIA GRIECCI & SPIKE
PARTY PLANNER FOR DOGS

"Parties are part of our family traditions and since my dog is part of my family, I want to include him in my traditions to show my love."

PATRICIA'S TIP: "A pawfect dog party needs a beginning, middle, and an end. Pass out doggy bags with party favors at the end of your party."

IDEAL DOGS FOR THIS ACTIVITY:

If you don't know your dog's birth date, celebrate her adoption date.

RESOURCES

Agility
American Kennel Club (AKC):
  akc.org
American Mixed Breed
  Obedience Registration
  (AMBOR): ambor.us
Canadian Kennel Club (CKC):
  www.ckc.ca
North American Dog Agility
  Council (NADAC):
  nadac.com
Say Yes! Dog Training:
  clickerdogs.com
The Kennel Club UK:
  thekennelclub.org.uk
United Kennel Club (UKC):
  ukcdogs.com
United States Dog Agility
  Association (USDAA):
  usdaa.com

Animal Actor
101 Dog Tricks:
  101dogtricks.com
American Humane Association:
  americanhumane.org
Birds and Animals Unlimited:
  birdsandanimals.com
Hollywood Paws Animal Career
  Academy and Pet Agency:
  hollywoodpaws.com
Le Paws Animal Talent Agency:
  lepawsagency.com
Moorpark College:
  moorparkcollege.edu
USDA Animal Exhibitor: aphis.
  usda.gov/animal_welfare/

Animal Communicator
Dr. Med. Vet. Isabelle Annette
  Schmid, PHD: xinli.ch
The Gurney Institute of
  Animal Communication:
  gurneyinstitute.com

Baton Jumping
101 Dog Tricks:
  101dogtricks.com

Bikejoring
See Sled Dog Racing

Blood Donor Dog
Animal Blood Bank:
  animalbloodbank.com
Dog Blood Donors:
  dogblooddonors.com

Canicross/ Caniteering
See Sled Dog Racing, also:
Canicross Trailrunners UK:
  canicross.org.uk
CaniX UK: cani-cross.co.uk
European Cani-Cross Federation
  (ECF): ecf.cc

Canine Ambassador
American Kennel Club (AKC):
  akc.org

Canadian Kennel Club (CKC):
  www.ckc.ca
The Kennel Club UK:
  thekennelclub.org.uk

Canine Good Citizen
American Kennel Club (AKC):
  akc.org
Canadian Kennel Club (CKC):
  www.ckc.ca
The Kennel Club UK:
  thekennelclub.org.uk

Canines at Prayer
Hawaii Kotohira Jinsha–Hawaii
  Dazaifu Tenmangu:
  e-shrine.org

Clicker Train
Karen Pryor Clickertraining:
  clickertraining.com

Companion Dog Show
Companion Dog Club:
  companiondogclub.org.uk
Nuts for Mutts: thewalk.
  nutsformutts.org
Scruffts Dog Show:
  scruffts.org.uk

Conformation Dog Show
Afterglow Kennel:www.
  afterglowshowdogs.com
American Kennel Club (AKC):
  akc.org
Canadian Kennel Club (CKC):
  www.ckc.ca
Crufts Dog Show: crufts.org.uk
The Kennel Club UK:
  thekennelclub.org.uk
United Kennel Club (UKC):
  ukcdogs.com
Westminster Kennel Club Dog
  Show:
  westminsterkennelclub.org
World Dog Show sponsored
  by Fédération Cynologique
  Internationale (FCI): fci.be

Creative Grooming
Barkleigh Productions:
  barkleigh.com
Intl. Judges Assoc. for Dog
  Grooming Competition:
  ijaonline.com

Dock Diving
Dock Dogs: dockdogs.com
Splash Dogs: splashdogs.com
Ultimate Air Dogs:
  ultimateairdogs.net
United Kennel Club (UKC):
  ukcdogs.com

Dog Camp
Iron Dogs Training Camp:
  iron-dogs.com
Say Yes Dog Training Camp:
  clickerdogs.com

Dog Carting
See Sled Dog Racing, also:
Canadian Kennel Club (CKC):
  www.ckc.ca
Nordkyn Outfitters:
  nordkyn.com
Sacco Dog Carts: uninor.no

Dog Model
See Animal Actor, also:
Jilli Dog: JilliDog.com
Pet Fashion Week:
  petfashionweek.com

Dog Scouts
Dog Scouts: dogscouts.org

Dog Trainer
Animal Behavior
  College (ABC):
  animalbehaviorcollege.com
Animal Behavior Society:
  animalbehavior.org
Association of Pet Dog Trainers
  (APDT): apdt.com or
  apdt.co.uk
Certified Applied Animal
  Behaviorists (CAAB):
  certifiedanimalbehaviorist.com
Dog Star Daily:
  DogStarDaily.com
International Association of
  Canine Professionals (IACP):
  canineprofessionals.com
International Dog School:
  internationaldogschool.com
Karen Pryor Academy:
  KarenPryorAcademy.com
Moorepark College:
  moorparkcollege.edu
National Association of Dog
  Obedience Instructors, Inc.
  (NADOI): nadoi.org
National K-9: nk9.com
Patricia McConnell:
  patriciamcconnell.com
Tom Rose Dog Training
  Academy: tomrose.com
Triple Crown Academy for
  Professional Dog Trainers:
  schoolfordogtrainers.com

Dog Trick Contest
101 Dog Tricks:
  101dogtricks.com

Doga
Barking Buddha:
  brendabryan.net

Doggy Birthday Party
PlayMore Publishing:
  playmorepublishing.com

Dogrobatics
Sundance Dog Team:
  sundancedogteam.com

Drag Hunting
The Masters of Draghounds and

Bloodhounds Association:
  mdbassociation.co.uk

Earthdog
American Kennel Club (AKC):
  akc.org
American Working Terrier
  Association (AWTA):
  dirt-dog.com
Canadian Kennel Club (CKC):
  www.ckc.ca
Jack Russell Terrier Club of
  America (JRTCA): terrier.com
Missouri Earthdogs (MOE):
  moeearthdogs.org
The Kennel Club UK:
  thekennelclub.org.uk
United Kennel Club (UKC):
  ukcdogs.com

Fetch
See books on page 207

Field Retrieving
American Kennel Club (AKC):
  akc.org
Canadian Kennel Club (CKC):
  www.ckc.ca
Hunting Retriever Club (HRC):
Martin Deeley:
  martindeeley.com
National Shoot to Retrieve
  Association (NSTRA):
  nstra.org
North American Hunting
  Retriever Association
  (NAHRA): nahra.org
North American Versatile
  Hunting Dog Association
  (NAVHDA): navhda.org
United Kennel Club (UKC):
  ukcdogs.com

Flyball
Australian Flyball Association
  (AFA): flyball.org.au
British Flyball Association
  (BFA): flyball.org.uk
North American Flyball
  Association (NAFA):
  flyball.org
United Flyball League
  International (U-FLI): u-fli.org

Flygility
New Zealand Flygility Dog
  Association/ National Agility
  Link Association (NALA):
  nala.org.nz
New Zealand Kennel Club
  (NZKC): nzkc.org.nz

Flying Disc
Flying Disc Dog Open (FDDO):
  fddo.org
Skyhoundz: skyhoundz.com
The UFO: ufoworldcup.org
The US Disc Dog Nationals
  (USDDN): usddn.com

Flying Dog
Hausi the flying dog:
perufly.com/hausi

Foster a Dog
American Society for the
Prevention of Cruelty to
Animals (ASPCA): aspca.org
Humane Society of the United
States: animalsheltering.org
Jin-Sohl Jindo Dog Rescue:
jindo-dog-rescue.org

Freestyle Disc
Skyhoundz: skyhoundz.com
The UFO: ufoworldcup.org
The US Disc Dog Nationals
(USDDN): usddn.com

Geese Wrangler
Geese Police, Inc.:
geesepolice.com

Guide Dog Puppy Raiser
Canine Companions for
Independence (CCI):
caninecompanions.org
Guide Dogs for the Blind:
guidedogs.com
International Guide Dog
Federation (UK):
ifgdsb.org.uk

Hand Signals
Standard hand signals for all
tricks are shown in "101 Dog
Tricks" page 207

Herding
American Herding Breed
Association (AHBA):
ahba-herding.org
American Kennel Club (AKC):
akc.org
Australian Shepherd Club of
America (ASCA): asca.org
Canadian Kennel Club (CKC):
www.ckc.ca
International Sheep Dog Society
(ISDS) Great Britain:
isds.org.uk
Task Farms: taskfarms.org
The Kennel Club UK:
thekennelclub.org.uk
United States Border Collie
Handler's Association
(USBCHA): usbcha.com

High Jump
Soaring Cindy:
soaringcindy.com

Hiking and Camping
Hike With Your Dog:
hikewithyourdog.com
National Park Service: nps.gov

Homemade Dog Treats
Three Dog Bakery:
threedog.com

Hoop Jumping
Busy Bee Dog Productions:
busybeedogs.com

Hound Trailing
Border Hound Trailing
Association (BHTA):
borderhoundtrailing.com
Department for Environment
Food and Rural Affairs, UK
(DEFRA): defra.gov.uk
Hound Trailing Association
(HTA): houndtrailing.org.uk
Lakeland Trailhound Welfare:
trailhoundwelfare.org.uk

Hydrotherapy
Association of Canine Water
Therapy:
caninewatertherapy.com
La Paw Spa: lapawspa.com
The Canine Hydrotherapy
Association:
canine-hydrotherapy.org

Jog a Shelter Dog
Get Fit with Fido:
getfitwithfido.org
Jog the Dogs: www.tulsaspca.org

Junior Handler
See each dog sport, also:
Young Kennel Club UK (YKC):
ykc.org.uk

K9 Drill Team
Southern Golden Retriever
Society Display Team:
southerngoldenretriever.com

Kayaking
Dog Souts of America:
dogscouts.org

Land Mushing
See Sled Dog Racing

Literacy Dogs
Intermountain Therapy Animals:
therapyanimals.org

Long Jump
Purina Incredible Dog
Challenge: purina.com

Look-Alike Contest
Check local listings

Lure Coursing
American Kennel Club (AKC):
akc.org
American Sighthound Field
Association (ASFA): asfa.org
Canadian Kennel Club (CKC):
www.ckc.ca
Fédération Cynologique
Internationale: fci.be
National Greyhound Association
(NGA): ngagreyhounds.com

Massage
Equisage: equissage.com
Tellington TTouch Training:
ttouch.com

Messenger Dog
Svenska Brukshundklubben
Swedish Working Dog
Association:
brukshundklubben.se
Swedish Kennel Club: skk.se

Musical Canine Freestyle
Canine Freestyle Federation:
canine-freestyle.org
Canine Freestyle GB:
caninefreestylegb.com
Heelwork to Music GB:
heelworktomusic.co.uk
Musical Dog Sport Association:
musicaldogsport.org
Paws 2 Dance Canine Freestyle
Organization:
paws2dance.com
Paws n Music Association:
paws-n-music.co.uk
The Kennel Club UK:
thekennelclub.org.uk
World Canine Freestyle
Organization:
worldcaninefreestyle.org

Muskrat Racing
Missouri Earthdogs Club:
moearthdogs.org

Obedience Competition
American Kennel Club (AKC):
akc.org
American Mixed Breed
Obedience Registration
(AMBOR): ambor.us
Canadian Kennel Club (CKC):
www.ckc.ca
National Association of Dog
Obedience Instructors
(NADOI): nadoi.org
The Kennel Club UK:
thekennelclub.org.uk
United Kennel Club (UKC):
ukcdogs.com

Off-Leash Dog Park
Cesar Millan: cesarsway.com
Dog Park USA: dogparkusa.com

Pawprint Memory Stone
Paw Print Kit:
milestonesproducts.com

Pawprint Painting
Paw Posies: pawposies.com

Pet Detective
Kat Albrecht: katalbrecht.com
Missing Pet Partnership:
missingpetpartnership.org
Pet Detective Training:
petdetectivetraining.com

Pet Parade
Barkus Mardi Gras parade for
dogs, New Orleans: barkus.org
Beggin' Strips Barkus Pet
Parade: beggintime.com or
mardigrasinc.com
Woofstock Pet Fair:
woofstocknorcal.com

Phodography
Nick Saglimbeni, Slickforce
Studio: slickforce.com
Professional Photographers of
America: ppa.com

Physically Challenged Dogs
DogKarts: dogkarts.com

Handicapped Pets:
handicappedpets.com

Pointing Game Bird
American Kennel Club (AKC):
akc.org
Canadian Kennel Club (CKC):
www.ckc.ca
Jim's Bird Dog Training:
jimsbirddogtraining.com
North American Versatile
Hunting Dog Association
(NAVHDA): navhda.org
United Kennel Club (UKC):
ukcdogs.com

Puppy Class
STAR Puppy: akc.org/starpuppy

Rally-O
American Kennel Club (AKC):
akc.org
American Mixed Breed
Obedience Registration
(AMBOR): ambor.us
Association of Pet Dog Trainers
(APDT): apdt.com
Canadian Kennel Club (CKC):
ckc.ca
Canine Work and Games
(C-Wags): c-wags.org
United Kennel Club (UKC):
ukcdogs.com

Rope Jumping
Extreme Canines Stunt Dog
Show: stuntdog.com

Scent Detection Work
K9 Nose Work:
k9nosework.com
National Association of Canine
Scent Work (NACSW):
nacsw.net
Snifferdog Sport:
snifferdogsport.com

Scent Hurdle Racing
Canadian Kennel Club (CKC):
www.ckc.ca

Schutzhund
American Working Dog
Federation (AWDF): awdf.net
Continental Kennel Club:
continentalkennelclub.com
Deutscher Verband der
ebrauchshundsportvereine
(DVG): dvgamerica.com
Fédération Cynologique
Internationale (FCI): fci.be
German Shepherd Dog Club
of America-Working Dog
Association (GSDCA-WDA):
gsdca-wda.org
Schutzhund Training:
schutzhund-training.com
The Kennel Club:
thekennelclub.org.uk
United Kennel Club (UKC):
ukcdogs.com
United Schutzhund Clubs
of America (USA):
germanshepherddog.com

Verband für das Deutsche
Verband für das Deutsche
Hundewesen (VDH): vdh.de
Von Der Wilmothhaus German
Shepherds of Distinction:
wilmothdogs.com

Scootering
See Sled Dog Racing

Search and Rescue
American Rescue Dog
Association: ardainc.org
National Association for Search
and Rescue (NASAR):
nasar.org
National Disaster Search
Dog Foundation:
searchdogfoundation.org
National Search and Rescue
Dog Association (NSARDA):
nsarda.org.uk
North American Search Dog
Network (NASDN): nasdn.org

Service Dog
Assistance Dogs
International (ADI):
assistancedogsinternational.org
Canine Partners for
Independence:
caninepartners.co.uk
Delta Society: deltasociety.org
International Association of
Assistance Dog Partners
(IAADP): iaadp.org
People's Dispensary for Sick
Animals (PDSA): pdsa.org.uk

Skateboard
Tyson the Bulldog:
skateboardingbulldog.com

Skijoring
See Sled Dog Racing, also:
Skijor Now: skijornow.com

Skimboard
Tillman the Dog:
youpet.com/tillman

Sled Dog Racing
Alaskan Malamute HELP
League: malamuterescue.com
Alpine Outfitters:
alpineoutfitters.net
Dog Powered Scooter:
dogpoweredscooter.com
Dogs Across America:
www.dogsacrossamerica.org
European Sled Dog Racing
Association: esdra.net
FidoGear: fidogear.com
Iditarod Trail Sled Dog Race:
iditarod.com
International Federation of
Sleddog Sports:
sleddogsport.com
International Sled Dog Racing
Association: isdra.org
Mush with Pride:
mushwithpride.org
Mushing Magazine:
mushing.com
Run Dawg Run:

rundawgrun.com
Sled Dog Central:
sleddogcentral.com
Snowpaw store:
snowpawstore.com

Soccer
Soccer Collies:
soccercollies.com

Spa Day / Grooming
Pet Stylist: petstylist.com
Rescue® Remedy:
rescueremedy.com

Stand-Up Paddleboard
Holua Stand-Up Paddleboards:
holua.com

Stunt Dog Show
Extreme Canines Stunt Dog
Show: stuntdog.com
Sundance Dog Team:
sundancedogteam.com
USDA Animal Exhibitor:
www.aphis.usda.gov/
animal_welfare/

Surfing
Coronado Surfing Academy:
coronadosurfing.com
Loews Surf Dog Competition:
LoewsSurfDog.com
San Diego Dog
Surfing Association:
sandiegodogsurfing.com
Surfin Paws: surfinpaws.com

Swimming
See Hydrotherapy

Teaching a Deaf of Blind Dog
Amazing Aussies, Phoenix AZ:
amazingaussies.com
Kooper at Kooper's World:
koopersworld.com

Terrier Hurdle Racing
Jack Russel Terrier Club
of America (JRTCA):
therealjackrussell.com
United Kennel Club (UKC):
ukcdogs.com

Tetherball
See books on page 207

Therapy Dog
Delta Society: deltasociety.org
Therapy Dogs International:
tdi-dog.org
Therapy Dogs, Inc.:
therapydogs.com

Tracking
American Kenel Club (AKC):
ack.org
Canadian Kennel Club (CKC):
www.ckc.ca
The Kennel Club UK:
thekennelclub.org.uk

Truffle Snuffling
Fiera Nazionale del Tartufo
Bianco d'Alba, International
White Truffle Fair of Alba,
Italy: fieradeltartufo.org

Mycorrhizal Systems Truffle
Dog Training School, Truffle
Hunting Championships,
Hampshire England:
plantationsystems.com
North American Truffle
Grower's Association
(NATGA™):
trufflegrowers.com
African truffles:
AfricanTruffles.com
The Great British and Irish
Truffle Association
(G.B.I.T.A.): GBITA.com

Ugly Dog Contest
Check local listings

Volunteer Dog Patrol
Lake Metroparks:
lakemetroparks.com
Volunteer Trail Safety Patrol,
East Bay Regional Park
District: parkpatrol.org

Water Rescue
Canine Water Sports:
caninewatersports.com
Dog Scouts: dogscouts.com
Newfoundland Club of America:
ncanewfs.org
Portuguese Water Dog Club of
America: pwdca.org

Weave Pole Racing
Clean Run Ultimate Weave Pole
Challenge: cleanrun.com
Purina Incredible Dog Challenge
(PIDC): purina.com

Weight Pulling
American Pulling Alliance:
weightpull.com
Canadian Kennel Club (CKC):
www.ckc.ca
International Sled Dog Racing
Association: isdra.org
International Weight Pulling
Association: iwpa.net
United Kennel Club (UKC):
ukcdogs.com
United Pulling Federation:
upfweightpull.webs.com

Wallace the Pit Bull:
wallacethepitbull.com

Whistle Train
Hubert Bailey's Border Collies:
bordercollies.net
See also herding

Wiener Dog Racing
Dachshund Club of America:
dachshund-dca.org
The National Dachshund Races:
weinerrace.com
The Wienerschnitzel Wiener
Nationals: holidaybowl.com
Wiener Tales: wienerraces.com

Wildlife Conservation Work
Department of Natural Resources
(specific to each state)
Report a found banded bird:
reportband.gov
The Nature Conservancy:
nature.org
U.S. Fish & Wildlife Service:
fws.gov
U.S. Geological Survey:
usgs.gov
Working Dogs for
Conservation (WDC):
workingdogsforconservation.org

Windsurf
Sevin the water dog:
mauiwindcam.com
The Gorge in Hood River:
windsurf.gorge.net

Youth Dog Project
4-H: 4-h.org
4-H World Atlas:
www.national4-hheadquarters.
gov/about/4h_atlas.htm
National Collegiate 4-H
organization: collegiate4h.org

IN MEMORIAM: Before this book went to print, two special dogs passed away.Our dogs fill our hearts when they are with us and then, for a while, our hearts are broken when they leave us. But they will always live n in a space reserved for them in our heart. Chihuahua "**Cricket**" (page 193) was a dog actor with a big personality in a tiny body. American Staffordshire terrier "**QT**" (page 179) was a registered therapy dog who brought joy to the hospital patients he visited.

PHOTOGRAPHER CREDITS

Photography by Christian Arias for SlickforceStudio with the exception of the following:

AFP/Getty Images, 78; 194 (top); 156 (top); 198

Dale Andreoli, 105 (top)

Apple Tree House/Getty Images, 140

Associated Press, 36; 56; 76 (top); 94; 138; 158 (top); 177 (top); 180; 190 (top); 191 (top); 195 (bottom)

© Gonzalo Azumendi/agefotostock.com, 42 (top)

Ingrid Bahlenberg, 28–29

Hubert Bailey, 111 (top)

Raymond Beal, 153 (top)

© Vicki Beaver/Alamy, 168

Mark E. Beckloff, 199, Top

© Lee Beel/Alamy, 114 (top)

Nic Berard, 141 (bottom)

Dennis Betts, 131 (top)

Jo Anna Birmingham, 197 (top)

Kim Boyles, 21 (bottom)

Liz Breault/Shoot the Breeze PhotoWorks, 97 (top)

Stefani Brendl, 174; 175 (top)

Mike Brenson, 169 (top)

Rick Caran, 156 (bottom)

Ryan Cardone/Tidal Stock, 69

chuckgoodenough.com, 106 (bottom)

Jim Crosthwaite, 157 (bottom)

Don Davis Photography © 2002, 88 (bottom)

Marion Dean, 81

Martin Deeley/floridadogtrainer.com, 117

Sam Deltour, 42 (bottom)

Dog Scouts of America, 109 (bottom); 194 (middle & bottom)

www.dogshelpkids.org, 181

Steven Donahue/See Spot Run Photography, 98

Claire Doré, 148 (bottom)

Due South, 21 (top, inset)

Jamie Lu Dunbar, 141 (top)

Donna Dustin, 92–93

© Thorsten Eckert/agefotostock.com, 182

Diane Edmonds/eppicsurf.com, 67

Patricia A. Etherington, 186 (bottom)

Molly Feeney, 123 (top)

Frank Fennema Photography/FrankFennema.com, 60

Fly Above All Paragliding, 175 (middle, top & middle)

Turner Forte/Getty Images, 64

Peter Franke, 45 (bottom)

Andreas Fuhrmann/zumapress.com, 91 (top)

Susan Garrett, 13 (top)

Kathy Keatley Garvey/University of California, Agriculture & Natural Resources, 126

Dan Gauss, Shot On Site Photography, 22

Getty Images, 48; 50; 72; 136; 148 (top); 163 (top & bottom)

Heather Gilfillan, 188–189

Svitlana Gilyun, 59 (top)

www.grafichouse.co.uk, 74

Spencer Grant/zumapress.com, 178

Joshua J. Grenell, 57 (top)

Patricia Griecci, 201 (bottom)

Haley Harland, 25 (bottom)

Sandy Hartness, 165

Jill Hayes Photography, 30, 31 (top); 32

P. J. Heller/zumapress.com, 104

Karen Hocker Photography, 12

Courtney Huther, 125 (top)

© imagebroker/Alamy, 45 (top)

Shirley Indelicato, 129 (top)

iStockphoto.com, 89 (top); 176 (top)

Marysia Jastrzebski, 77 (top)

© Mark A. Johnson/Alamy, 70 (top)

© Juniors Bildarchiv/agefotostock.com, 52

© Jupiterimages/agefotostock.com, 201 (top)

Donna Kelliher Photography, 130

Carole Kelly, 179 (top)

The Kennel Club Picture Library, 110; 144; 150

Terry Kenney, 137 (top)

The Kern County Fire Department/Edwina Davis, 86; 87

Nannette Klatt, 183

Bonita Knickmeyer, 24 (bottom)

Shirley LaMear, 89 (bottom)

Simon Lamen, 51 (top)

www.lapawspa.com, 76 (bottom)

Pam Lauritzen, petstylist.com, 170 (bottom)

Loews Coronado Bay Resort, 66

Los Alamitos Race Course, 25 (top)

Mark Lukas, 107

Krys Lumsden, 58

Photo by Lunen Dogs, 17 (top)

Lana Maeder, 35 (top)

David Marcks & Diane Nevaras/Geesepolice.com, 139

Katherine Martucci, 106 (top)

Ray Masters, 70 (bottom)

Kendall McMinimy/Getty Images, 162

Andrew Sánchez Meador, 120 (bottom)

© Melba Photo Agency/Alamy, 80

Milestonesproducts.com, 196

Raymond Miller, 53

Laura Mitobe, 44 (bottom)

Mark Muir, 99 (top)

Ren Netherland, 164

Alicia Nicholas, 15 (top)

Joel Norton, 113 (top)

Debbie O'Brien, 27

Laura O'Neill, 101

Lonnie Olson, 65

onEdition/www.w-w-i.com/crufts, 146

Nadja Palenzuela, 73 (top); 114 (bottom)

Allen Parton/The Kennel Club Picture Library, 184

Pawposies.com, 195 (top)

Chris Perondi/www.stuntdog.com, 14; 160; 161

Trish Perondi, 37 (top)

© Mike Perry/Alamy, 16

Mary Ray, 143 (top)

Rich Reid/Getty Images, 172

© Rich Reid Photography.com, 173

Nick Ridley/nickridley.com, 20 (top); 116

Nichole Royer, 43

Nick Saglimbeni/www.slickforce.com, 8; 34; 107 (bottom); 113 (bottom); 197 (bottom)

Joel Sartore/Getty Images, 90

Marc Saunders, 75

Alan Sawyer, 26

Dr. Isabelle Schmid, Ph.D., 121 (bottom)

Mark Schneider, St. Louis, MO, 157 (top)

J. Gerard Schwerdt, 79

Maria Scott, 120 (top)

Joy Leilei Shih, 61 (top)

Shutterstock.com, 132

Marshall Smith, 100

Judi Snowdon, 21 (bottom, inset)

Charles Snyder/MyTrial/Photos.com, 133 (top)

Steve Southard, 128

Bev Sparks, www.dogphotography.com, 166–167

Genniper Stemplewski, 191 (bottom)

© Stockbroker/agefotostock.com, 186 (top)

Justin Sullivan/Getty Images, 24 (top)

Kyra Sundance, 39 (top); 41 (top); 44 (top); 91 (bottom); 108; 111 (bottom); 127; 176 (bottom); 199 (middle); 200 (bottom)

Aleksandra Szydlowska, 151

Irene Takizawa, 177 (bottom)

Kim Tinker, 49 (top)

Christine Titus, 187 (bottom)

The Tulsa SPCA/Pat Atkinson, 187 (top)

Tom Uhlman Photography/tomuphoto.com, 109 (top)

© UK21/Alamy, 96

Michael Uy, 2; 175 (bottom)

Svetlana Valoueva, 147

A.Van Kampen/The Kennel Club Picture Library, 82

Matilda van Rijnberk/equinepictures.net, 20 (bottom)

www.w-w-i.com/crufts, 142

Lisa Wallgren, 83

Brandon Waring, 190 (bottom)

Thomas Wasper, 192

Hardin Weaver, 88 (top)

Stewart Weller, © 2007, 145

www.wikipedia.org, 185

Jim Wilson, 23 (top)

Bettina Woolbright Photography, 77 (bottom)

ACKNOWLEDGMENTS: Thanks to **Heidi Horn** (production assistant, bandanna coordinator, dog petter, and Kyra's mother), **Claire Doré** (dog wrangler), and my own Weimaraners **Chalcy** and **Jadie**. Thanks to all the beautiful dogs who participated in the studio photoshoots: **Cricket** (Chihuahua), **Skippy** (Jack Russell terrier), **Iris** (terrier mix), **Owen** (golden retriever), **Jiggs** (dalmatian), **Thunder** (Great Dane/boxer), **Caralot Aussies** (Australian shepherd puppies), **Charlie** (Afghan hound), **Mona** (German shepherd dog), **Hera** (English bulldog), **Jackson** (yellow shepherd mix), **Kwin** and **Jeep** (Alaskan malamutes), **Soon Hee** (jindo), **Bella** (Rottweiler), **Bullet** (Australian cattle dog), **Lola** (rough collie), **Flash** (McNab), and **Torch** (McNab puppy). Thanks to **Holua** stand-up paddleboards. Thanks to the dog trainers, competitors, and dog lovers who contributed their personal stories to this book. Your stories brought the book to life and will inspire others to do more with their dogs!

101 DOG TRICKS

STEP-BY-STEP ACTIVITIES TO ENGAGE, CHALLENGE, AND BOND WITH YOUR DOG

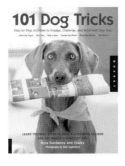

This international bestseller is the industry standard training book for adult dogs. Difficulty ratings range from "easy" to "expert" and "build-on" ideas suggest more complicated tricks which build on each new skill. If you want to teach your dog to *find the remote, carry your purse, play basketball,* and *jump rope,* then this is the book for you!

THE DOG TRICKS AND TRAINING WORKBOOK

A STEP-BY-STEP INTERACTIVE CURRICULUM TO ENGAGE, CHALLENGE, AND BOND WITH YOUR DOG

Track your progress as you work through this comprehensive curriculum. *Review* and *re-evaluation* sections at the end of each chapter prompt you to reflect on your progress and your improving relationship with your dog. *It also includes* 30 trick cards and a DVD.

51 PUPPY TRICKS

STEP-BY-STEP ACTIVITIES TO ENGAGE, CHALLENGE, AND BOND WITH YOUR PUPPY

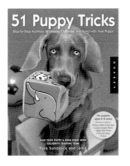

By teaching your puppy early and using positive reinforcement methods, you will instill in her a cooperative spirit and a lifetime love of learning. Especially for puppies ages birth to 2 years. It includes: *ring a bell to go out; loose-leash walk; wipe your paws;* and *fetch.*

THE DOG RULES

14 SECRETS TO DEVELOPING THE DOG YOU WANT

Simple behavior modification techniques such as "Focus on the Solution, Not the Problem," and "One Command, One Consequence," empower owners with a clear strategy. The Dog Rules does not involve intimidation nor escalating corrections but rather fosters a joyful relationship with a dog who balances enthusiasm with self-control.

BEST OF 101 DOG TRICKS (DVD)
BEST PUPPY TRICKS (DVD)

STARRING KYRA SUNDANCE

These award-winning DVDs feature step-by-step instruction and real world examples of training a novice dog. The **Puppy Tricks DVD** contains 17 tricks including *Spin Circles, Open the Door, Close the Door, Roll Over, Ring a Bell to go Outside, Wipe your Paws, Turn on the Tap Light,* and *Fetch.* The **Dog Tricks DVD** contains 16 tricks including *Say Your Prayers, Jump Through My Circled Arms, Shake Hands, Crawl, Beg, Take a Bow, Cover Your Eyes,* and *Tidy Up Your Toys.*

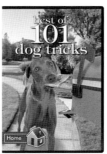

ABOUT THE AUTHOR

KYRA SUNDANCE is a world-acclaimed stunt dog show performer, dog trainer, and internationally bestselling author. Her dog team performs live acrobatic shows on premier stages internationally, at circuses, professional sports halftime shows, and on movies and television shows such as *The Tonight Show, Ellen, Entertainment Tonight, Worldwide Fido Awards, Animal Planet, Showdog Moms & Dads,* and *Beverly Hills Chihuahua 2.* Kyra and her dogs starred in Disney's *Underdog* stage show and in a command performance at the palace in Marrakech for the King of Morocco.

Kyra has written numerous popular dog training books including the international bestselling *101 Dog Tricks,* and hosts a line of award-winning dog training DVDs. She also set-trains dog actors for movies and TV and lectures on positive dog training methods.

Kyra is an avid sportswoman, a marathon runner, gymnast, and worked as a windsurfing instructor for Club Med. She is nationally ranked in competitive dog sports, having trained, competed, and titled in a great number of the sports featured in this book.

Kyra holds the human-dog bond at the heart of her training method. She cares for her dogs with tenderness, trains them thoroughly, and inspires them to excel. Her methods foster confident, happy dogs who are motivated to do the right thing rather than ones fearful of making a mistake. She shows us how to develop joyful relationships with dogs who balance enthusiasm with self control.

Kyra and her Weimaraners Chalcy and Jadie live with Kyra's husband on a ranch in California's Mojave desert. www.kyra.com

www.domorewithyourdog.com

Do More With Your Dog!